T0195799

WORD SEEDS THAT PRODUCE FAITH AND REMOVE FEAR, DOUBT, AND UNBELIEF

WHAT IS THE WORD SAYING TO YOU?

DR. BRENDA F. GRAHAM

WESTBOW
PRESS®
A DIVISION OF THOMAS NELSON
& ZONDERVAN

Copyright © 2023 Dr. Brenda F. Graham.

All rights reserved. No part of this book may be used or reproduced by any means, graphic, electronic, or mechanical, including photocopying, recording, taping or by any information storage retrieval system without the written permission of the author except in the case of brief quotations embodied in critical articles and reviews.

This book is a work of non-fiction. Unless otherwise noted, the author and the publisher make no explicit guarantees as to the accuracy of the information contained in this book and in some cases, names of people and places have been altered to protect their privacy.

WestBow Press books may be ordered through booksellers or by contacting:

WestBow Press
A Division of Thomas Nelson & Zondervan
1663 Liberty Drive
Bloomington, IN 47403
www.westbowpress.com
844-714-3454

Because of the dynamic nature of the Internet, any web addresses or links contained in this book may have changed since publication and may no longer be valid. The views expressed in this work are solely those of the author and do not necessarily reflect the views of the publisher, and the publisher hereby disclaims any responsibility for them.

Any people depicted in stock imagery provided by Getty Images are models, and such images are being used for illustrative purposes only. Certain stock imagery © Getty Images.

ISBN: 978-1-6642-9797-5 (sc)
ISBN: 978-1-6642-9798-2 (hc)
ISBN: 978-1-6642-9799-9 (e)

Library of Congress Control Number: 2023907198

Print information available on the last page.

WestBow Press rev. date: 06/05/2023

Scripture quotations are from the Holy Bible, King James Version (Authorized Version). First published in 1611. Quoted from the KJV Classic Reference Bible, Copyright © 1983 by The Zondervan Corporation.

Scripture taken from The Holy Bible, The ESV® Bible (The Holy Bible, English Standard Version®). ESV® Permanent Text Edition® (2016). Copyright © 2001 by Crossway, a publishing ministry of Good News Publishers. The ESV® text has been reproduced in cooperation with and by permission of Good News Publishers. Unauthorized reproduction of this publication is prohibited. All rights reserved.

Scriptures marked as NLT are taken from the Holy Bible, New Living Translation, copyright © 1996, 2004, 2015 by Tyndale House Foundation. Used by permission of Tyndale House Publishers Inc., Carol Stream, Illinois 60188. All rights reserved.

Scripture marked NKJV are taken from the New King James Version®. Copyright © 1982 by Thomas Nelson. Used by permission. All rights reserved.

Scripture marked NIV are taken from the Holy Bible, New International Version®. NIV®. Copyright © 1973, 1978, 1984 by International Bible Society. Used by permission of Zondervan. All rights reserved.

Scripture taken from the Amplified Bible (AMP), Copyright © 2015 by The Lockman Foundation, La Habra, CA 90631. All rights reserved.

Scripture taken from the Amplified Bible Classic Edition (AMPC), Copyright © 2015 by The Lockman Foundation, La Habra, CA 90631. All rights reserved.

Scripture taken from the NEW AMERICAN STANDARD BIBLE®, Copyright © 1960,1962,1963,1968,1971,1972,1973,1975,1977,19 95 by The Lockman Foundation. Used by permission.

Scripture taken from the Common English Bible®, CEB® Copyright © 2010, 2011 by Common English Bible.™ Used by permission. All rights reserved worldwide. The "CEB" and "Common English Bible" trademarks are registered in the United States Patent and Trademark Office by Common English Bible. Use of either trademark requires the permission of Common English Bible.

CONTENTS

FOREWORD

There is a fight taking place within our faith. Some have even pondered over the question of how? How does one keep moving when their faith is under attack? Oftentimes, our identities are diminished through the testing of trials. We all encounter rains, floods, and winds that attempt to disturb the integrity of our foundations. It is time to wake up! Strengthen what remains and is about to die, for our deeds have been found unfinished in the sight of God. *In Word Seeds That Produce Faith and Remove Fear, Doubt, and Unbelief,* Dr. Brenda F. Graham teaches the believer how to persevere through times of uncertainty.

We must fight strenuously for the defense of our faith. Jude 3:3 declares, "Beloved, when I gave all diligence to write unto you of the common salvation, it was needful for me to write unto you, and exhort you that ye should earnestly contend for the faith which was once delivered unto the saints" (KJV). We have to stand firm and remain rooted in Gospel truths. From the foundation of the earth, our identities preceded us. First Peter 2:9 declares, "But ye are a chosen generation, a royal priesthood, an holy nation, a peculiar people; that ye should shew forth the praises of him who hath called you out of darkness into his marvelous light."

Dr. Graham understands the gift of faith and how to use it. This thought-provoking manual will take the reader on a spiritual journey toward wholeness. It will uncover and embody principles of faith that are essential for spiritual growth. You will learn how to put faith into action through the full meaning of Word seeds. As you read this manual, I pray that God will give you understanding in all things.

—Shirene Hicks, pastor, prophetess, advocate, author

Shirene Hicks founded and established Breaking Through Barriers Ministries in 2014. She graduated from Living Word School of Ministry in 2017, received her ministerial licensing in 2017, and was ordained as a pastor under Dr. Bill Winston's Faith Ministries Alliance in 2020. Pastor Hicks earned a Master of Arts degree in pastoral counseling from Loyola University Chicago. She also earned a Master of Science degree in administration from Calumet College of St. Joseph. She is the author of 365 *Days of Tears*. She is also a sergeant of police and has worked as a law enforcement officer for two decades. Pastor Hicks enjoys traveling, reading, and spending time with her husband, Maurice, and the couple's three children.

ACKNOWLEDGMENTS

This manual is dedicated to my parents, Eunice, and Dorothy Williams. The years of sacrifice, guidance, encouragement, and support they gave me were instrumental in guiding my Christian life and providing me with a strong faith foundation. Both parents have gone to be with the Lord. However, their lives were examples of loving God, blessing their neighbors and friends, and encouraging their children to be disciplined, hardworking, consistent in good character, and people of excellence. My father shared his faith in quietness. That quietness taught me discipline, kindness, fortitude, insight, and how to love unconditionally.

I would like to thank my daughter Ms. Brittany Hernandez for her assistance in editing this book and making important suggestions that were useful in refining the message. Her expertise in writing was invaluable throughout the process. Additionally, her second pair of eyes allowed my vision to shine through, pushing me to strive for clarity and excellence.

I would like to thank my daughter Alsera for always believing in me and for all of her support and love during my many times of need. She has given me wonderful, loving grandsons, who have always made me feel loved, special, and cared for.

My son Marcus is a positive influence in my life. He is trustworthy and kind. Importantly, he makes me smile when I am around him. His presence always reminds me of what is important in life.

My daughter Tangela is a positive influence in my life. She is an innovative and visionary entrepreneur with great business and marketing skills. Her love for the Lord and her conscious efforts to allow the Holy Spirit to work through her have powerfully impacted her life and those around her.

My siblings, Evester Darrough (passed away in 2008), Dr. Bettye Williams, Shirley Williams, Dr. Margarette Williams, Charles Williams (passed away in 2015), N. Lucille Gilkey, Sterlin Williams, Ted Williams, Robin Baylark, and Sonnya Adams, have shared their lives with me and have always been invaluable mentors. I am privileged to have them in my life.

Lastly, I would like to thank all of the spiritual leaders and mentors who throughout my life have shared the message of love and grace with me and others. Their teachings have picked me up when I was in dark places, extended grace in times of need, and provided me with a spiritual foundation that will be with me as I continue my journey here on earth.

INTRODUCTION

The Bible is a book of scriptures. God speaks His truth to man in human words, or Word Seeds. First Peter, chapter 1, verse 23 testifies that Christians are "born again, not of corruptible seed, but of incorruptible, by the Word of God, which liveth and abideth forever." The seed is the Word of God. That means the Word of God is the life-giving power that is at work in the lives of born-again believers to stimulate spiritual growth and development. Importantly, God's Word has the power within itself to "reproduce" and bear fruit. The fruit contains seed that is programmed to prosper and bring forth more fruit.

Word Seeds have answers to any situation that may arise in the life of the believer. The answer is immediate in some situations. However, some seeds may need time to grow in others. This requires faith. Faith comes by hearing, and hearing by the Word of God (Romans 10:17). Word Seeds have the power to impact those who receive them by faith; they inform them and transform them into His image. Jesus said His Words were "spirit and life" (John 6:63). Studying and meditating on the Word of God, along with confessing Word Seeds, produce faith. Acting on faith produces a positive outcome. Storing the Word Seeds establishes deep faith. This is confirmed in the principle of seedtime and harvest: "While the earth remaineth, seedtime and harvest, and cold and heat, and summer and winter, and day and night shall not cease" (Genesis

8:22). The meaning in this instance is that Word Seeds have to be planted and watered, through reading, meditation, praise, and seeking God, until a harvest comes.

Because the Word of God is seed, it is always looking for a place to be planted, and knowledge of who God is provides revelation of His Word that releases supernatural energy and provides power to rise above challenges in life. The chapters in this manual contain information that reveal how to plant Word Seeds in the heart to produce spiritual illumination, drive away sin and darkness, supply continuous light to the soul, heal the body, emotions, and mind, and impart power and ability to rise above circumstances.

Blessings to you as you prepare to continue building your strong faith. It is needful that you have a regular, daily time with the Lord, seeking Him and His ways through His Word and interacting with Him in prayer and thanksgiving. The power of the Holy Spirit will be present to guide you into the truths of His Word.

HOW TO USE THIS MANUAL

This is not a book that you will read from page to page. Rather, it is a manual, or a guide, that will help you understand the full meaning of Word Seeds found in the Bible. The information presented in this book does not provide a full dissertation on each topic. Rather, a guide is presented that will lead you to seek further insights from the Lord. You will be led to pursue the full meaning of each topic through the anointing of the Holy Spirit as He leads you into fuller depths and deeper understanding of the topics.

All pronouns that refer to God are capitalized in this manual. This is a matter of the author's personal conviction and preference. The pronouns are capitalized to emphasize the context in which the statement is written and to make it clear that the reference is to the Lord. Some of the quoted Bible versions use pronouns that refer to God. Others do not. No changes are made to the different Bible versions.

The Bible is a book of words that represent God's will for mankind. God speaks His truth to man in human words, or Word Seeds. The chapters in this manual contain information that will reveal how to plant Word Seeds in the heart to produce spiritual illumination, drive away sin and darkness, supply continuous light to the soul, heal the body, emotions, and mind, and impart power and ability to rise above circumstance.

Chapter 1 presents an overview of the power of the Word of God in creation, the manifestation of His Son (Jesus Christ) as the Word in the first chapter of John, and the seeds of the Word (Word Seeds) that are planted in the heart to produce discipleship, knowledge, revelation, divine power, and faith in Jesus Christ. A discussion on the topics of faith, fear, doubt, and unbelief shows the impact of allowing fear, doubt, and unbelief to overwhelm faith and how those negative influences can be overcome by focusing and meditating on the Word of God.

Chapter 2 provides an overview of the importance of meditation and prayer in developing strong faith in God's Word. It includes examples of ways to meditate and a thorough explanation of how to meditate on the Word of God.

Chapter 3 offers a brief overview of the names of God and describes His attributes and characteristics. Word Seeds that provide knowledge of God, give insight into His highest spiritual privileges, discuss His divine power, and give an opportunity for salvation are discussed in detail.

Chapter 4 examines God's plan of salvation in Jesus Christ and reviews the various terms included in the salvation process. Word Seeds on the topics of forgiveness, repentance, grace, peace, fruit bearing, the newness of life, the sufficiency of Christ, faith, redemption, and righteousness are provided for meditation and spiritual edification.

Chapter 5 covers the topic of spiritual maturity and spiritual growth by elaborating on the roles of regeneration, transformation, and crucifying the flesh in the life of the believer. Word Seeds that discuss the roles of meditating and feeding on God's Word, being obedient to God's Word, resisting temptation, living sanctified lives, conquering the flesh, walking in the Spirit, planting godly seed, conquering the enemy, and becoming more Christlike are placed in this chapter.

Chapter 6 presents information on spiritual warfare and winning spiritual battles. Word Seeds that fight spiritual battles and remove fear, doubt, and unbelief are included in the chapter.

Chapter 7 provides Word Seeds that provide peace and healing in challenging times and situations.

Word Seed topics are included in Chapters 3-7. Each Word Seed topic contains the following:

- a descriptive subject
- Word Seed (key scripture)
- the seed of the Word
- the action of the Word
- the persistence of the Word
- scriptures for meditation
- a question: what is this Word saying to you?

Word Seed Topic and Key Scripture

The key scripture (Word Seed) comes before each passage to assist in understanding the topic that is addressed. It is usually highlighted throughout the discussion of the passage. However, other scriptures related to the topic provide spiritual context for the reader.

The Seed of the Word

The Bible contains God's Word. The words are living and perform supernatural acts (Hebrews 4:12). They make us wise unto salvation (2 Timothy 3:15). The Word is a seed. And because it is a seed, it is able to regenerate and grow, causing the reader to receive wisdom, revelation knowledge, and understanding.

Read the information in this section and ask yourself, "What is the Lord saying to me? If this is true, what does it mean for my life? What should I do about what I am learning?" If needed, go back to the information in chapter 3 and ponder the nature, character, and name (s) of God, determining how they are related to the information you are reading. Ask the Holy Spirit to lead and guide your heart as you meditate and muse over the topic.

The Action of the Word

God is living. Life consists of actions. God's actions are consistent and righteous. When God said, "Let there be light," light appeared (Genesis 1:3). Most important, the living Word is written to prosper in you and to produce fruit in you as you believe it, speak it, and act on it. Jesus said that the scriptures testify concerning Him. They reveal God, but they also give you a revelation of who you are. Study the key scripture and meditate on the additional scriptures as you allow the Holy Spirit to lead and guide you through the faith process. You must believe God's Word in order to receive from Him.

The Persistence of the Word

When we are persistent, we inherit the promises of God. When we meditate on the Word day and night, we prosper and succeed in all we do (Joshua 1:8). The important thing is that we do not become weary or tired, for God's Word says that we will reap if we do not give up (Galatians 6:9; Luke 11:9–10).

How is the Word Seed persistent? Our prayers are not always immediately answered or acted upon by God. However, He does hear our prayers, and His answers always bless us because He acts according to His will and plan. Persevering and continually trusting in Him is essential.

The persistence passages in each topic provide additional context for each topic. They are to remind you that the Lord gives us all that we need to receive His blessings.

What Is This Word Saying to You?

This question can be answered through study, possibly in the form of reflection through meditation. The focus in chapter 3 is on knowing God. That includes knowing His names, characteristics, and attributes, His works, promises, ways, and purposes. That is to say, we are engaging in an activity that will consciously bring the presence of God before us so that we can get to know Him better, experience His goodness, bask in His love, feel the warmth and comfort of His glory, and learn His ways.

Here is a small list of some of the ways this can be accomplished:

- Rewrite the topic in your own words and include a description of what you are saying.
- Determine if the topic is speaking to a certain area in your life. Did you learn anything? If so, discuss what you learned from the study.
- Memorize key verses.
- Take notes while you are studying.
- Use other scripture references (Bible dictionaries, concordances, different Bible versions, other books or articles related to the topic) to assist you as you reflect on the topic.
- Frame a spiritual learning principle from the information.

Blessings to you as you prepare to continue building your strong faith. It is needful that you have a regular, daily time with the Lord, seeking Him and His ways through His Word and interacting with Him in prayer and thanksgiving. The power of the Holy Spirit will be present to guide you into the truths of His Word.

1

THE WORD IS GOD

G OD'S SPOKEN WORD CREATED THE WORLD AND EVERYTHING IN it (Genesis 1:1–3). He spoke, and things came into existence that were not previously there. The first words in the Bible were "In the beginning" (Genesis 1:1a). This scripture confirms that the world was empty and void before creation: "And the earth was without form, and void; and darkness was upon the face of the deep." Word Seeds form the explicit written representation of God that is spoken in the Bible. The Word teaches us who God is and communicates His plans and purposes for humankind. Christian life is guided by the truths expressed throughout the Bible.

The Word of God is seed. The term *Word Seeds* will be used to describe God's Word throughout this manual. God speaks His truth to humans in human words, or Word Seeds. Word Seeds have answers to any situation that may arise in the life of the believer. They have the power to influence those who receive them by faith by informing them and transforming them into God's image. Jesus said His words were "spirit and life" (John 6:63). That means the Word of God is the life-giving power that is at work in the lives of born-again believers to stimulate spiritual growth and development. Thus, God's Word has the power within itself to reproduce and bear fruit.

Fruits contain seeds that are programmed to prosper and bring forth more fruit. The Word Seeds provide answers to situations that arise in the life of the believer. Studying and meditating on the Word of God, along with confessing Word Seeds, produce faith. The answer is immediate in some situations. However, some seeds may need time to grow. This requires faith. "Faith comes by hearing, and hearing by the Word of God" (Romans 10:17).

The plan of salvation is revealed in the Old and New Testaments of the Bible. Included is deliverance from sin and death through repentance and faith. The message of faith and deliverance is revealed in the Old Testament in the calling of Abraham, the deliverance of the Israelites, and God's faithfulness and care for them. God made Himself known in the presence of Jesus Christ, the incarnate Word in the New Testament. Jesus is presented as the source of salvation for all humankind in many passages within the Bible. He fulfilled the law, and through Him grace and truth are available to all who believe in Him through God's Word.

Grace is given in response to the initiative from God to believe in His Son, who was born as a man to give His life on the cross as a sacrifice for the sins of humankind and to bring them into fellowship with the Father. As a result of the sacrifice of Jesus Christ, we do not have to offer animals sacrifices to be saved from our sins. Jesus gave us eternal fellowship with God. The purpose of His death resounds throughout the Old and New Testaments. He died in our place to provide atonement and forgiveness and pay the penalty for our sins for the last time.

> Surely he hath borne our griefs, and carried our sorrows: yet we did esteem him stricken, smitten of God, and afflicted. But he was wounded for our transgressions, he was bruised for our iniquities: the chastisement of our peace was upon him; and with

his stripes we are healed. Yet it pleased the Lord to bruise him; he hath put him to grief: when thou shalt make his soul an offering for sin, he shall see his seed, he shall prolong his days, and the pleasure of the Lord shall prosper in his hand. (Isaiah 53:4–5, 10)

The first chapter of John summarizes the position of Jesus—the Word made flesh—and authenticates the fact that He is one with God. An understanding of several significant verses in the chapter will prove the reality of Jesus as the Word of God.

In the beginning was the Word, and the Word was with God, and the Word was God. The same was in the beginning with God. All things were made by him; and without him was not anything made that was. In him was life; and the life was the light of men. That was the true Light, which lighteth every man that cometh into the world. But as many as received him, to them gave he power to become the sons of God, even to them that believe on his name. And the Word was made flesh, and dwelt among us, (and we beheld his glory, the glory as of the only begotten of the Father,) full of grace and truth. (John 1:1–4, 9, 12, 14)

Verse 1 establishes that the Word was "in the beginning with God," and "the Word was God." The Greek term for "Word" is *logos*. The *Merriam-Webster* online dictionary[1] defines *logos* as "the divine wisdom manifest in the creation, government, and redemption of the world and often identified with the second person of the Trinity." Verse 2 continues the declaration that the Word (Jesus) was in the beginning with God. Verse 3 declares, "All things were made through him, and without him was not anything made that was made." This verse is saying that the Word (Jesus) was in the beginning and presented as the Creator of the "heavens and the earth." Verse 4 reveals the Word (Jesus) as the source of life: "In him was life, and the life was the light of men." We are reminded in verse 9 that Jesus is the "true light" or "the way, the truth, and the life" (John 14:6). Verse 12 proclaims that all who receive Christ through faith become children of God. And verse 14 gives us a clear picture of Jesus as the Word: "And the Word became flesh and dwelt among us, and we have seen his glory, glory as of the only Son from the Father, full of grace and truth."

Jesus is the manifold wisdom of God. Everything that God wants us to know concerning Him—including His will, acts, ways, promises, and plan of salvation—was manifested in Christ Jesus. He is the personal Word of God. The Word is piercing, active, and discerning. But it also brings life and healing to all who yield to it in faith.

> But of him are ye in Christ Jesus, who of God is made unto us wisdom, and righteousness, and sanctification, and redemption. (1 Corinthians 1:30)

The Word of God is the only way to the truth and meaning of life as designed by God. Significantly, the Word is living and the way by which God leads us to Him. The Word supplies our prayer lives with the wisdom, guidance, and strength to meet the conditions and circumstances that occupy our lives on a daily basis. Constantly feeding upon the Word of God through reading and meditation strengthens your prayer life. Most important, reading and feeding upon the Word produces faith (Romans 10:17). Knowing this principle is important because answers to prayers are related to the faith that we have when we pray.

For the word of God is full of living power. It is sharper than the sharpest knife, cutting deep into our innermost thoughts and desires. It exposes us for what we really are. (Hebrews 4:12 NLT)

The Call for Fellowship with God

God wants to have a relationship with His people. This means we are to always have a direct line of fellowship with Him. Fellowship means that we share our lives with God. We come to Him to commune and to express our joys and sorrows at any time of the night or day. However, fellowship is also sharing in the life of Christ. We share in His life when we share in His work and have a clear knowledge of His will. One of the most expressive chapters in the Bible concerning unity and fellowship with the Lord is found in John 15. Let us look at a portion of that scriptural text.

I am the true vine, and my Father is the husbandman. Every branch in me that beareth not fruit he taketh away: and every branch that beareth fruit, he purgeth it, that it may bring forth more fruit. Now ye are clean through the word which I have spoken unto you. Abide in me, and I in you. As the branch cannot bear fruit of itself, except it abide in the vine; no more can ye, except ye abide in me. I am the vine, ye are the branches: He that abideth in me, and I in him, the same bringeth forth much fruit: for without me ye can do nothing. (John 15:1–5)

God's desire is to be always with us, and Jesus is the way to that fellowship. It is essential to understand that fellowship and unity cannot be accomplished unless the participants have like interests and possess common purposes and feelings. In effect, fellowship with God is keeping His commandments. When we fellowship with God "as the branches," He becomes our source of life, and we begin to produce fruit of the Spirit. Producing fruit means we have the life-flowing channels of love, peace, longsuffering, gentleness, goodness, faith, meekness, and temperance. Fellowship with God is essential to this fruitfulness (Galatians 5:22–23).

Prayer and Faith in God's Word

Faith increases when we hear or read the Word of God. This is important because prayer must be aligned with faith. For that reason, time must be spent in the Word of God so that faith will be increased for the purpose of prayer. When that happens, God expresses His love for us by answering our prayers, because He wants our faith in Him to increase. Importantly, He wants us to know and understand the goodness, the love, and the kindness of His grace toward us. God is always ready to answer prayers of faith.

Prayer expresses dependence on God; it requires sincerity, repentance, purpose, and fellowship. When we fellowship with God, we also fellowship with the Son and the Holy Spirit, because these three are one. More on this topic will be discussed in chapter 3. We must approach the Lord in faith, believing that He is a rewarder of those who seek Him with all their hearts (Hebrews 11.6).

If we don't believe that God will answer our prayers when we pray, then prayer becomes meaningless. We can compare it to "sounding brass or a tinkling cymbal," as Paul did in 1 Corinthians 13:1, when he spoke of the meaningless of gifts and prophecies that were given without love. However, if we know that God answers prayers and that our lives are in conformity with His Word, then we know that He hears us when we pray "the effectual, fervent prayer of a righteous man availeth much" (James 5:16b KJV).

The Bible (Word) is a witness of God's grace and loving kindness. More importantly, we learn who we are in Christ, because studying the Bible reveals who God is, teaches us how to obey Him, and shows us how to love one another. The outcome is that we become more like Jesus. Everything in our lives—those who are impacted by us and our communities—will be positively affected by our lives.

The Word is also a representation of God's plan for the salvation of man through Jesus Christ. Knowledge of this principle brings more meaning into our prayer lives because we know and can confirm that what the Word says is true. The Word of God also teaches us that daily fellowship with God through prayer and reading or hearing His Word brings victory and power into our lives, because the Holy Spirit communicates with our natural spirit. We become one with God.

Knowledge of God's Word also provides the confidence to pray for us as well as for others. It accomplishes all that God intended (Isaiah 55.11). The results will become meaningful because we know that He will hear and answer our prayers. This should result in a transformed life, a life that reflects Christ. The confidence to pray and believe that the impossible will be carried out will transform the prayer life (Isaiah 55:11).

> "If My people who are called by My name will humble themselves and pray and seek My face and turn from their wicked ways, then will I hear from heaven and will forgive their sin and will heal their land" (2 Chronicles 7.14).

The very existence of prayer and meditation is dependent upon the will of God as expressed through His Word. Meaningful prayer has no standing outside the revelation of God's will as expressed through the scriptures. God wants us to seek His will and purpose for our lives. The Word transforms our minds and wills and therefore our hearts and minds. We then become vessels of honor, sanctified and ready to be used by Him.

The Word of God as Seed

Jesus compared the Word as seed in the parable of the sower. This parable is found in Mark 4:1–9 and Mark 4:13–20. The parable describes what happens when a farmer sows seeds in various types of soil. The seed represents the Word of God that is sown as the Gospel. The soil represents the response of different hearts to the Gospel, and the sower is the one who proclaims the Gospel. The parable will be discussed later in the chapter.

What Is a Seed?

The *Britannica Dictionary*[3] defines a seed as a small object produced by a plant, from which a new plant can grow. Seeds contain genetic material that, when released into a suitable environment, produce offspring of its own kind. When you inspect seeds from the outside, they appear hard, dry, or without life. However, if placed in the proper soil and environmental condition, a seed will begin to stir, germinate, and bring forth new life. From that definition and personal knowledge of seeds, we can understand that a single seed holds all the reproductive needs that can be transferred to offspring, meaning the seed has all the genetic information needed to reproduce itself. A seed is a copy of the plant that produced it.

Jesus said that the Word of God was like a seed. The parallel is that the Word has the power to grow or cause growth to happen.

If it is planted within an obedient and receptive heart, the Word should reproduce itself. Christianity has survived for over two thousand years because of the procreative power of scripture. God's Word is omnipotent and persistent. It is all-powerful, supreme over everything, and unfailing in its strength and capacity.

Natural Seed Requirements for Growth

The natural resources and conditions needed for plant growth include an adequate water supply; a light source; soil in which to grow; time for proper development, growth, and maturity; and an optimal temperature maintained throughout growth. Heslop-Harrison[3] described the conditions and elements needed to sustain germination. Each is discussed briefly below.

1. *Water* is essential to both the life and the growth of a plant. Seeds absorb and are filled up with water to germinate. Some seeds need to be immersed in water to germinate. This hydration process is needed to start the activities involved in the germination process. They include the formation of protoplasm, or the living substance needed for plant growth; the dissolving of oxygen throughout the embryo; the softening of the coat of the seed; and increased seed permeability or penetration.

2. *Light* starts the signal to begin the germination process in plants. Light, whether from the sun or an artificial light source (such as a lightbulb), gives the small plant the energy it needs to begin photosynthesis. Photosynthesis is the process the plant uses to convert light energy into food. Light also assists the forming plant which way is up and where to send its leaves to receive light for it to produce its own food.

3. *Proper soil* provides the nutrients needed for germination. Soil nutrient is important. The better the soil, the healthier and stronger the plant. Some nutrients needed for plant growth include magnesium, calcium, and phosphorus.

4. *Time* represents the period it will it take for the seed to germinate under ideal conditions. Different plants require various times for plant growth.

5. *Temperature* is important because seeds only germinate when the environment is conducive to ideal temperature. Most plants grow best when the daytime temperature is about ten to fifteen degrees higher than the nighttime temperature. Under these conditions, plants photosynthesize (build up) and respire (break down) during optimum daytime temperatures and then curtail respiration at night.

Word Seed

The Lord established the principle of seedtime and harvest when He created the earth. Seedtime represents the time seeds are planted, and harvest is the season in which they are reaped. This is true in the spiritual realm as well as in the physical realm. The seeds that we plant from the Word of God produce a harvest in our lives. Seeds grow up and reproduce themselves when planted. The Word of God is seed that produces His will. The seed grows up after it is planted. A growth period takes place between the time it is planted and the time it yields fruit. This is the law of seedtime and harvest. It has been around since its creation.

> As long as the earth endures, seedtime and harvest, cold and heat, summer and winter, day and night will never cease. (Genesis 8.22 NIV)

Apostle Peter likened seed to the Word of God in 1 Peter 1.23 (NKJV): "Having been born again, not of corruptible seed but incorruptible, through the word of God which lives and abides forever." Seeds look dormant but are alive on the inside. God's Word is alive. They may seem lifeless and difficult to read for some. However, they are full of life.

> "It is the Spirit who gives life; the flesh profits nothing. The words that I speak to you are spirit, and they are life." (John 6.63 NKJV)

The Word of God produces nothing if it is not planted. It must be planted in the heart and mind to be productive. After it is planted, it must grow and conceive or give birth. New birth cannot take place without planting and nourishing the seed. This process is achieved by reading and speaking the Word into your life and being obedient to what it says. Meditating, thinking about the Word, and reciting it help plant it in our hearts. This is not always an overnight process. It might take days, weeks, months, or years for the Word to become fully matured in the heart.

God's Word contains His promises. It is good to hear others teach and preach the Word. However, the harvest will be more bountiful if it is planted in the heart by speaking and hearing it individually as well. As the seed grows and matures, the promises of God manifest as actions and blessings. Persistently affirming the Word is essential if we are going to keep and guard the Word in our hearts. Those affirmations will produce promotions, prosperity, healing, peace, security, and protection if they are constant companions (Joel 3:10).

> Let us hold fast the confession of our hope without wavering, for He who promised is faithful. (Hebrews 10.23)

The Parable of the Sower

> Behold, a sower went out to sow. And it happened, as he sowed, that some seed fell by the wayside; and the birds of the air came and devoured it. Some fell on stony ground, where it did not have much earth; and immediately it sprang up because it had no depth of earth. But when the sun was up it was scorched, and because it had no root it withered away. And some seed fell among thorns; and the thorns grew up and choked it, and it yielded no crop. But other seed fell on good ground and yielded a crop that sprang up, increased, and produced: some thirtyfold, some sixty, and some a hundred. And He said to them, "He who has ears to hear, let him hear." (Mark 4:3–9 NKJV)

The Parable of the Sower Explained

Jesus described the main roles in this parable. They are the sower (spreads or plants the Word), the seed (the Word of God), and the soil (the condition of the human heart). In the parable, a farmer scatters seeds, which fall in four different places: a road, rocky soil, soil infiltrated by thorny weeds, and good soil. The seeds on the road were eaten by birds and never had a chance to grow. The seeds on the rocky soil came up rapidly but withered in the sun because they did not have enough soil to take root. The seeds in the weeds were overcome by thorns that choked and overtook them. The seeds that fell upon good ground and fertile soil grew strong and produced good fruit (Mark 4:13–20).

Understanding the Parable of the Sower

The Lord compares your heart to a garden (Jeremiah 31:12). If you plant the right seeds, you will bring forth good fruit—some thirty, some sixty, and some a hundredfold. Different people will produce different levels of fruit in their lives. The seed is always the same, the Word of God. The condition of the heart is what differs. That is what determines the amount of seed that will be produced. The individuals representing various types of soil (the conditions of their hearts) had varying results. The individuals representing the first type of soil characterized those who were not ready to receive the Word, which is the Good News of God. They immediately rejected it when it was given, because their hearts were hardened, seduced by Satan, and fixed on earthly things. The second set of individuals represented soil that was rocky and unable to be turned over. At first, they were overjoyed with excitement and emotions. However, they did not give the Word the opportunity to take root. Due to the lack of depth, the trials and persecutions of the world caused them to fall away. The main reason for falling away was not taking the time to study the Word or to seek God further. The third group of individuals represented soil that was in competition with the world. The individual heard the Word, but the cares of the world and the deceitfulness of riches became their undoing. The Word was choked out of them, and they became unfruitful. The last group represented good soil. The individual not only heard the Word but also understood and obeyed it, causing fruit to bear. The amount of fruit received represented the amount of time attending to the Word of God. Some yielded a hundredfold, some sixty, and others thirty.

Faith, Fear, Doubt, and Unbelief

Faith is a product of a relationship with God, knowledge of His Word, and the indwelling presence of the Holy Spirit in one's life. Romans 10:17 says, "So then faith comes by hearing, and hearing by the word of God." The principle is this: What you hear goes into your mind. If you meditate and dwell on it, it goes into your heart. From your heart, it goes to your mouth. When you speak your heart, you hear your heart. If the Word is what is in your heart, the result is increased faith because you hear the Word. The fact that it is your mouth speaking what you hear is irrelevant. The Word produces faith regardless of who speaks it.

Fear

We are reminded in 2 Timothy 1:7 that fear does not come from the Lord. Fear in that passage, according to Strong's Concordance, [2] means "timidity, fearfulness, and cowardice." This is speaking of a fear that is dominating and controlling a person's life to the degree that they allow it to rule their thoughts and control their decision-making.

Fear is always of the mind. It is not a concrete or physical substances that has the ability to overtake or control. It is developed as a result of a thought process that causes and triggers the fight-or-flight response in a person. All of this happens in the mind. It can be overcome, meaning that thinking differently about a situation can remove fear. The key to overcoming fear is to understand what we focus on determines how we feel. Whatever we focus on is what we are going to feel. Developing and practicing a mindset that substitutes thoughts of fear with thoughts of God's Word will provide an alternative to fear. Feelings of fear imply that the seed of God's Word has not been planted in the heart.

"Fear does not come from God; and He does not want us to be in fear." The Bible says that fear has torment (1 John 4:18). It shackles and keeps one's desires and dreams from coming into fruition. It also keeps one from enjoying life to the fullest and causes irrational thinking along with unhappiness. Philippians 4:6 reminds us to pray and entreat the Lord when attacked by fear. Two additional verses are useful to meditate on when approached by fear.

> In peace I will both lie down and sleep, for You, Lord, alone make me dwell in safety and confident trust. (Psalm 4:8 AMP)

> Yes, though I walk through the [deep, sunless] valley of the shadow of death, I will fear or dread no evil, for You are with me; Your rod [to protect] and Your staff [to guide], they comfort me. You prepare a table before me in the presence of my enemies. You anoint my head with oil; my [brimming] cup runs over. (Psalm 23:4–5 AMP)

Doubt

The definition of doubt in the online version of the *King James Bible Dictionary*[5] states, "To waver or fluctuate in opinion; to hesitate; to be in suspense; to be in uncertainty." In summary, doubt means to waiver on opinions concerning the Word of God. In the context of this topic, it means "to be double-minded," proving that both seeds of faith and seeds of unbelief have been planted and are striving in the heart. A double-minded person believes God one minute and begins to unbelieve the next time. The seed of doubt can be watered with knowledge of the Word of God that is received through meditation and the power of the Holy Spirit watering the heart. The disciple Thomas, who is sometimes called Doubting Thomas, was in disbelief when he was told that Jesus had risen from the dead.

> Now Thomas (also known as Didymus), one of the Twelve, was not with the disciples when Jesus came. So the other disciples told him, "We have seen the Lord!" But he said to them, Unless I see the nail marks in his hands and put my finger where the nails were, and put my hand into his side, I will not believe." A week later his disciples were in the house again, and Thomas was with them. Though the doors were locked, Jesus came and stood among them and said, "Peace be with you!" Then he said to Thomas, "Put your finger here; see my hands. Reach out your hand and put it into my side. Stop doubting and believe." Thomas said to him, "My Lord and my God." (John 20:24–29 NIV)

As we meditate on this Word, we can determine that Thomas was absent when Jesus appeared and showed Himself to the other disciples. His doubting was based upon the fact that he did not see Christ and needed more proof. He received that proof when Jesus appeared to him a while later. As He had done with the other disciples, Jesus showed Thomas his scars as a proof of life (John 20:27). Thomas said, "My Lord and my God!" (John 20:28). We can determine from this passage that the light of the Word (Christ) removes darkness and reveals Him to us, as with Thomas.

Another example of doubt is found in Matthew 21:18–22, in the parable of the fig tree.

And when he saw a fig tree in the way, he came to it, and found nothing thereon, but leaves only, and said unto it, Let no fruit grow on thee henceforward forever. And presently the fig tree withered away. And when the disciples saw it, they marveled, saying, How soon is the fig tree withered away! Jesus answered and said unto them, Verily I say unto you, If ye have faith, and doubt not, ye shall not only do this which is done to the fig tree, but also if ye shall say unto this mountain, Be thou removed, and be thou cast into the sea; it shall be done.

Jesus was standing on the Mount of Olives as He was speaking. It may seem from the natural point of view that He was referring to a natural mountain. However, He was referring to any problem or obstruction that comes before us. He followed that statement by saying that faith is what is needed to remove barriers in our lives. That kind of faith knows the omnipotence and power of God, a faith that can only know Him through a knowledge of His Word.

We can locate another situation that may have caused doubt in the hearts of the disciples when He said, "Destroy this temple, and in three days I will raise it up" (John 2:19). It took forty-six years for the Israelites to build the temple. How could Jesus raise it up again in three days? They possibly doubted and certainly misunderstood what He was saying at the time He said it. They readily understood when He rose from the death of the cross after three days.

Jesus answered and said unto them, Destroy this temple, and in three days I will raise it up. Then said the Jews, Forty and six years was this temple in building, and wilt thou rear it up in three days? But he spoke of the temple of his body. When therefore he was risen from the dead, his disciples remembered that he had said this unto them; and they believed the scripture, and the word which Jesus had said. (John 2:19–22)

Unbelief

The biblical meaning of unbelief, as derived from scripture, means refusing to believe in God and His Word. It comes from a lack of faith or believing something other than what God says about a situation. The Bible calls this "an evil heart of unbelief and departing from the living God" (Hebrews 3:12). Unbelief hinders you from receiving God's promises (Hebrews 3:19). It also hinders His works from being achieved. Jesus did not do miracles in Nazareth because of the lack of belief of the people who lived there (Matthew 13.58). The important thing to realize is that unbelief can be overcome by knowledge of the Word of God (Romans 10.17).

The Seed of God's Word in Our Hearts Helps to Overcome Fear, Doubt, and Unbelief

The seed of all scripture must be planted into our lives if we are going to grow spiritually. The Word of God helps us to experience salvation at its fullness. You cannot grow spiritually without it. The Old Testament prepares the heart and mind for the coming Christ. The New Testament reveals Christ as the Center of Deity. "For in Him dwells all the fullness of the Godhead bodily" (Colossians 2.9). Jesus made it clear that he did not come to condemn mankind but rather to bring abundant life and freedom from the oppression of sin, Satan, and a world in opposition to God's truth and goodness.

> For God did not send his Son into the world to condemn the world, but to save the world through him. (John 3:16–17 NIV).

You may believe in God, but if you are filled with unbelief regarding the promises in His Word, you will miss many great spiritual blessings. The Word of God has power to set us free from sin, doubt, and deception. God does not wish to leave us in spiritual darkness unto our own ignorance and unbelief. He is always ready to give His light, wisdom, and truth to all who seek Him and who hunger for His Word. Through the gift of the Holy Spirit, He helps us to grow each and every day in faith, knowledge, and understanding of His life-giving Word.

> All Scripture is inspired by God and is useful to teach us what is true and to make us realize what is wrong in our lives. It corrects us when we are wrong and teaches us to do what is right. God uses it to prepare and equip his people to do every good work. (2 Timothy 3:16–17 NIV)

> Like newborn babies, you must crave pure spiritual milk so that you will grow into a full experience of salvation. (1 Peter 2:2 NLT)

2

MEDITATING ON THE
WORD OF GOD

Blessed is the man that walketh not in the counsel of
the ungodly, nor standeth in the way of sinners, nor
sitteth in the seat of the scornful. But his delight is in
the law of the Lord; and in his law doth he meditate
day and night. And he shall be like a tree planted by
the rivers of water, that bringeth forth his fruit in his
season; his leaf also shall not wither; and whatsoever
he doeth shall prosper.

—Psalm 1:1-3

MEDITATION IS REFLECTING UPON GOD'S WORD. *Vines Expository Dictionary of the New Testament*[6] defines meditation as (a) "to attend to, practice," 1 Timothy 4:15, "be diligent in" ("meditate upon"), to practice is the prevalent sense of the word;" (b) "to ponder, imagine," Acts 4:25."

This definition of meditation aligns with prayer, study, and the work of the Holy Spirit in our lives as we reflect on God's Word. Reflection assists in visualizing the Word of God and applying it to areas of our lives that need resolution. As we reflect on God's words, we become actively engaged with the Holy Spirit. He takes the Word, anoints us, and transforms our minds, wills, and emotions. When hearts and minds are turned to God's Word in response to life's circumstances, lives become aligned with the will and purpose of God. Spiritual forces of evil and worldly weapons will not be able to invade and take hold of those individuals. Significantly, our souls will become converted, and our minds, wills, and emotions will be transformed into God's likeness.

> And be not conformed to this world: but be ye transformed by the renewing of your mind, that ye may prove what is that good, and acceptable, and perfect, will of God. (Romans 12:2)

God's weapons are powerful because they are spiritual. They are listed in Ephesians 6:11–19 and 1 Thessalonians 5:8. The words in these scriptures include dedication to truth, righteousness, proclamation of the Gospel, faith, love, hope of salvation, the message of God, and persevering prayer.

> Put on the full armor of God so that you can take your stand against the devil's schemes. For our struggle is not against flesh and blood, but against the rulers, against the authorities, against the powers of this dark world and against the spiritual forces of evil in the heavenly realms. Therefore put on the full armor of God, so that when the day of evil comes, you may be able to stand your ground, and after you have done everything, to stand. Stand firm then, with the belt of truth buckled around your waist, with the breastplate of righteousness in place, and with your feet fitted with the readiness that comes from the gospel of

peace. In addition to all this, take up the shield of faith, with which you can extinguish all the flaming arrows of the evil one. Take the helmet of salvation and the sword of the Spirit, which is the word of God. And pray in the Spirit on all occasions with all kinds of prayers and requests. With this in mind, be alert and always keep on praying for all the saints. Pray also for me, that whenever I open my mouth, words may be given me so that I will fearlessly make known the mystery of the gospel. (Ephesians 6.11-19).

But since we belong to the day, let us be self-controlled, putting on faith and love as a breastplate, and the hope of salvation as a helmet. (1 Thessalonians 5:8)

Meditation and the Word of God

Pray without ceasing. In everything give thanks: for this is the will of God in Christ Jesus concerning you. Quench not the Spirit. (1 Thessalonians 5:17–19)

.

While a topic of dispute and discussion for centuries as for its intent, we see that "praying without ceasing" simply means that Christians should make prayer and meditation ongoing acts in their lives. It is as simple as being consciously or subconsciously always situated in the presence of God. To be precise, the spirit of the child of God should always be in alignment with God's Spirit. In order for this to happen, one must be positioned in prayer and, more importantly, the Word of God.

The challenge for many Christians is not just knowing how to meditate but also how to make unceasing prayer and meditation important daily. Significantly, fellowship with God develops from knowledge of and conformity to His will. That within itself defines submission. Submission comes from studying, reading, and meditating on the Word of God. John says it this way:

> That which was from the beginning, which we have heard, which we have seen with our eyes, which we have looked upon, and our hands have handled, of the Word of life … That which we have seen and heard declare we unto you, that ye also may have fellowship with us: and truly our fellowship is with the Father, and with his Son Jesus Christ. (1 John 1:1, 3)

You cannot have true fellowship with anyone unless you get to know him/her first by establishing some type of relationship. If continued, the relationship will form a bond between the two of you. The bond will link you together and forge an intimate connection. Intimacy forms due to reciprocal information that has been directly transferred from one to the other. This form of bonding grows and increases with time, knowledge, and mutual contact. Clearly this means that true fellowship with God comes through prayer and meditation that is built over time and is established with mutual sharing or reciprocity. Let us look at another passage of scripture.

> And he who searches our hearts knows the mind of the Spirit, because the Spirit intercedes for the saints in accordance with God's will. And we know that in all things God works for the good of those who love him, who have been called according to his purpose. (Romans 8:27–28)

Fellowship is an inward unity produced by the Holy Spirit to lead one to the Father. This suggests that the heart should be open to the presence and leading of God on an ongoing basis. The heart opens itself to the things of God. When the heart is opened to God, a direct line of communication forms between God and man. The line of communication is mutual and shared. You speak with God; He speaks with you. The approach can be both audible when you speak with God through words and phrases, as well as reflective, when you commune with Him meditatively. The indication is that prayer is reciprocal. The Holy Spirit is constantly present to lead and guide Christians into "all truth." Keep in mind that the line of communication is there for fellowship, instruction, and guidance. It allows the promises of God to become evident in the lives of Christians and opens a channel of contact to and from God.

> Howbeit when he, the Spirit of truth, is come, he will guide you into all truth: for he shall not speak of himself; but whatsoever he shall hear, that shall he speak: and he will shew you things to come. (John 16:13)

As previously established, prayer and meditation involve fellowship with God. We have also established that prayer and meditation come from spending time with the Holy Spirit and allowing Him to commune with us. After a few minutes, the dialogue may become monotonous or at best something that has been committed to memory over time. The challenge is hearing what the Lord is saying to you through His Word. The scriptures contain everything that is needed to answer any concern. The more constantly we feed on the Word, the richer and deeper our prayer and meditation lives will become. That is because the Word is the food that gives us the strength and ability to hear the Lord effectively.

God uses explicit statements in Psalm 19 to describe the Word. The Word is described as being able to "convert the soul, make wise the simple, rejoice the heart, enlighten the eyes, endure eternally, and being true and righteous altogether."

> The law of the Lord is perfect, converting the soul: the testimony of the Lord is sure, making wise the simple. The statutes of the Lord are right, rejoicing the heart: the commandment of the Lord is pure, enlightening the eyes. (Psalm 19:7–8)

God gave us His Word not only in written form but also in living form so that we could know Him, have a personal relationship with Him, and feed on His love. It is our living voice showing us the way to God. That relationship must be reciprocated through our acknowledgment of Him in our daily living, both in word and in action, as well as our communicating with Him through prayer and meditation.

> For the word of God is full of living power. It is sharper than the sharpest knife, cutting deep into our innermost thoughts and desires. It exposes us to what we really are. Nothing in all creation can hide from him. Everything is naked and exposed before his eyes. This is the God to whom we must explain all that we have done. (Hebrews 4:12–13 NLT)

Jesus is an excellent example of one who sought the Father constantly in prayer. His constant request involved seeking the Father's will. When He prayed in Gethsemane, "Yet not as I will, but as You will," and when a disciple asked Jesus, "Lord, teach us to pray" (Luke 11:1), He responded with the Lord's Prayer. The Bible also tells us to pray without ceasing (1 Thessalonians 5:17). This directive was also given by Jesus in Luke 18:1.

Persevering in prayer and faith protects us and keeps us safe from the evil, Satan, and his demons. Being purposeful in prayer is critical to being able to accomplish the will of God for our lives. Prayer offers fellowship with God and should be persistent. Importantly, the prayers of a righteous man or woman will bring needed help from God. It brings peace and comfort to the soul and protects one from evil influences.

> And shall not God avenge his own elect, which cry day and night unto him, though he bear long with them? I tell you that he will avenge them speedily. Nevertheless when the Son of man cometh, shall he find faith on the earth. (Luke 18:7–8)

> Confess your faults one to another, and pray one for another, that ye may be healed. The effectual fervent prayer of a righteous man availeth much. (John 5:16)

Scriptural Meditations: Building Strong Faith by Knowing God

Genesis 2:7 describes how God made Adam: "The Lord God formed the man of dust from the ground and breathed into his nostrils the breath of life." As heirs together with Jesus Christ, Christians enter an inheritance that consists of God's gift of Himself. God image will begin to reflect itself in our lives, because we have His nature in us. Revelation 21:3 says, "He will dwell with them, and they will be his people, and God himself will be with them as their God."

The Word of God testifies concerning God's plan and will for man. What does this mean for us? Since the scriptures testify concerning God, we should focus on Him when we read His Word and plant it in our hearts. God is not separated from His Word. Before reading or studying God's Word, we should pray and ask Him to help us understand what He is saying to us.

> "Study this Book of Instruction continually. Meditate on it day and night so you will be sure to obey everything written in it. Only then will you prosper and succeed in all you do." (Joshua 1:8 NLT)

These instructions from Joshua 1:8 came to Joshua as he was preparing to lead the Israelites into their Promised Land. The Lord's command to him was to study and meditate on His Word day and night. He also discussed the importance of being obedient to what was written in the Word: "Only then will you prosper and succeed in all you do."

As the Israelites approached the walls of Jericho in preparation for entering the Promised Land, Joshua was given implicit instructions, that they were to march around the wall for seven days and to carry the Ark of the Covenant with them. The Ark of the Covenant served as a religious symbol where the people could meet with God. The Lord hovered over the ark when the priests were present. If the priests were absent, the presence of the law tablets reflected His presence. Hebrews 9:4 verifies what items were inside the Ark of the Covenant. Behind the second curtain was a room called the Most Holy Place. It contained the golden altar of incense and the gold-covered Ark of the Covenant. The gold jar of manna, Aaron's staff that had budded, and the stone tablets of the covenant were also in the Most Holy Place.

Faith in God's Word will cause any walls that face His people to fall. We read in Joshua, chapter 6, verses 1 through 12, that the walls of Jericho fell on the seventh day of the march after they blew their trumpets as instructed. This left no doubt that the Lord was with them. Importantly, He honored the promise made to Joshua in Joshua 1:5–9:

> "No man shall be able to stand before you all the days of your life ... Be strong and courageous, for you shall cause this people to inherit the land that I swore to their fathers to give them ... Do not turn from it to the right hand or to the left, that you may have good success wherever you go ... Be strong and courageous. Do not be frightened, and do not be dismayed, for the LORD your God is with you wherever you go."

An Example of How You Can Meditate on a Scripture on Your Own or in a Group

> "For My thoughts are not your thoughts, Neither are your ways My ways," declares the LORD. "For as the heavens are higher than the earth, So are My ways higher than your ways, And My thoughts than your thoughts." (Isaiah 55:8)

Pray and seek the Lord for His anointing and listen closely to the Holy Spirit for guidance. Write this key scripture down and memorize it if you are led to do so. Then start pondering its words. Use different versions of the Bible, commentaries, concordances, and other scriptural references to gather information needed for your meditation. A review of this verse is discussed below. It will be reviewed phrase by phrase.

"For My thoughts are not your thoughts. Neither are your ways My ways"

Isaiah 55:8 is only one scripture out of a group of scriptures that have a common theme. Read verses 1 through 7 to assist in understanding verse 8. They describe how the Lord cried out to Israel to return to Him. He reminded them in verse 8 that He could supply all of their needs. This is where we will start. Our understanding of the names of God helps to understand that He is omnipotent, omniscient, sovereign, eternal, and all-knowing. He is eternal, and He knows the end from the beginning of all things. That means that He does not have to wonder how situations are going to turn out; He already knows. Importantly, all His acts are in alignment with His plans and ways. Nothing is impossible or without fulfillment with Him (Luke 1:37 AMP): "For with God nothing is ever impossible and no word from God shall be without power or impossible of fulfillment." Having that information should commit us to be obedient to the commandment of God found in Psalm 37:5: "Commit your way unto the Lord, and He shall bring it to pass. Whatever the Lord plans will come to pass. And whatever He purposes will come forth." Our responsibility is to commit our plans and ways to Him.

"Declares the LORD"

The Lord God is the sovereign ruler of heaven and earth. What He declares will come to pass. His ways are higher than man's. What He wills and says will come to pass; He is the Almighty God who watches over His Word to fulfill it (Jeremiah 1:12). "His Word accomplishes that which He pleases, and purposes and it prospers in the thing for which He sent it."

He declared His sovereignty to King Cyrus in Isaiah 46:9–11: "I am God, and there is no other; I am God, and there is none like me. I make known the end from the beginning, from ancient times, what is still to come. I say, 'My purpose will stand, and I will do all that I please.'"

"For as the heavens are higher than the earth, so are My ways higher than your ways and My thoughts than your thoughts."

The Lord reminds us that His thoughts and our thoughts are not the same, just as His ways are not our ways. He then reminds us of His promises by comparing the rain and precipitation of this earth to the promises He has made to us in His Word. His promises are not empty; they come to pass. Just as the rain provides the necessary water needed for plants and crop to grow, God's Word will achieve the purpose for which he sent it: "So shall my word be that goeth forth out of my mouth: it shall not return unto me void, but it shall accomplish that which I please, and it shall prosper in the thing whereto I sent it" (Isaiah 55:11).

3

KNOWING AND
RECEIVING FROM GOD

THE BIBLE TEACHES THAT THERE IS ONLY ONE GOD (ISAIAH
43:10). He is an existent and loving God who created man
to rule over and have dominion over the earth. He is a
sovereign Spirit who created heaven and earth. Having an intimate
knowledge of who God is gives us confidence in Him as the source
of our life and existence. No god was formed before Him, and no
god will ever take His place.

> Ye are my witnesses, saith the Lord, and my servant
> whom I have chosen: that ye may know and believe
> me, and understand that I am he: before me there
> was no God formed, neither shall there be after me.
> (Isaiah 43:10)

God manifests Himself in three divine persons, the Father, Son,
and Holy Spirit. The Bible teaches that the Father is God (Exodus
3:14), that Jesus is God (John 8:58), and that the Holy Spirit is God
(Acts 5:3–4). One clear statement of His existence as Father, Son,
and Holy Spirit is found in the fifth chapter of 1 John.

Whoever believes that Jesus is the Christ is born of God. Whoever loves the Father also loves the child who is born of him. By this we know that we love the children of God when we love God and keep his commandments. For this is the love of God, that we keep his commandments. His commandments are not grievous. For whatever is born of God overcomes the world. This is the victory that has overcome the world: your faith. Who is he who overcomes the world, but he who believes that Jesus is the Son of God? This is he who came by water and blood, Jesus Christ, not with the water only, but with the water and the blood. It is the Spirit who testifies because the Spirit is the truth. For there are three who testify in heaven: the Father, the Word, and the Holy Spirit; and these three are one. (1 John 5:1–7)

God the Father

God the Father refers to the first person in the Trinity, which also includes His Son, Jesus Christ, and the Holy Spirit. The Bible reveals God as "the God and Father of the Lord Jesus."

Blessed be the God and Father of our Lord Jesus Christ, who hath blessed us with all spiritual blessings in heavenly places in Christ. (Ephesians 1:3)

God is sovereign and in complete control of everything that happens in the world. Jesus explains His role as Father in John 14:6–11. Specifically, Jesus Christ, as God in the flesh, came to show us what God is like. He also declares that that the only way to the Father is through Him.

Jesus said to him, "I am the way, the truth, and the life. No one comes to the Father except through Me. "If you had known Me, you would have known My Father also; and from now on you know Him and have seen Him." Philip said to Him, "Lord, show us the Father, and it is sufficient for us." Jesus said to him, "Have I been with you so long, and yet you have not known Me, Philip? He who has seen Me has seen the Father; so how can you say, 'Show us the Father'? Do you not believe that I am in the Father, and the Father in Me? The words that I speak to you I do not speak on My own authority; but the Father who dwells in Me does the works. Believe Me that I am in the Father and the Father in Me, or else believe Me for the sake of the works themselves." (John 14:6–11)

In the Gospel of Matthew 6:9–13, Jesus teaches the Lord's Prayer to His disciples when one of them says, "Lord, teach us to pray." Many Christians have come to know and even memorize this prayer. The purpose of prayer is to show the supremacy of the Father, His place in our lives, and His place in our prayers. He is the Creator and ruler of everything. When we pray to Him as Father, we affirm His sovereignty, His majesty, His supremacy, His righteousness, and His authority.

"After this manner therefore pray ye: Our Father which art in heaven, Hallowed be thy name. Thy kingdom come, Thy will be done in earth, as it is in heaven. Give us this day our daily bread. And forgive us our debts, as we forgive our debtors. And lead us not into temptation but deliver us from evil: For thine is the kingdom, and the power, and the glory, forever. Amen." (Matthew 6:9–13)

Jesus Christ

Jesus Christ, or the "Son of God," was the fullness of the godhead bodily, "for in him dwelleth all the fulness of the Godhead bodily" (Colossians 2:9). The Bible continues this description of Jesus in Hebrews 1:3 and John 3:16.

> "Who being the brightness of his glory, and the express image of his person, and upholding all things by the word of his power, when he had by himself purged our sins, sat down on the right hand of the Majesty on high." As the only begotten Son of God, Jesus is co-equal with Him. (Hebrews 1:3)

> For God so loved the world, that he gave his only begotten Son, that whosoever believeth in him should not perish, but have everlasting life. (John 3:16)

Jesus was further described in Revelation 1:8 as the Lord God, "who is and was and who is to come, the Almighty." The Almighty title that is ascribed to Him declares Him to be our ruler who deserves our worship, obedience, submission, and worship. He has always existed and always will exist as the Almighty, who was in the beginning with the Father and Holy Spirit, to create everything.

> "I am Alpha and Omega, the beginning and the ending, saith the Lord, which is, and which was, and which is to come, the Almighty." (Revelation 1:8)

He was also revealed as the Word of God, who was in the beginning with God and was manifested in the flesh, as written in John 1:1–12 (NIV). This reference depicts Him as fully God, who was made man. He came to earth to die on the cross of Calvary and was raised again on the third day to save mankind from sin and to redeem him back to God, the Father.

> In the beginning was the Word, and the Word was with God, and the Word was God. He was with God in the beginning. Through him all things were made; without him nothing was made that has been made. In him was life, and that life was the light of all mankind. The light shines in the darkness, and the darkness has not overcome it. There was a man sent from God whose name was John. He came as a witness to testify concerning that light, so that through him all might believe. He himself was not the light; he came only as a witness to the light. The true light that gives light to everyone was coming into the world. He was in the world, and though the world was made through him, the world did not recognize him. He came to that which was his own, but his own did not receive him. Yet to all who did receive him, to those who believed in his name, he gave the right to become children of God. (John 1:1–12 NIV)

Jesus did not only make salvation available to man. He also made it possible for us to have a relationship with the living God through His resurrection and ascension to heaven to sit at the right hand of the Father. This places Him as head of the church.

For by Him all things were created that are in heaven
and that are on earth, visible and invisible, whether
thrones or dominions or principalities or powers. All
things were created through Him and for Him. And
He is before all things, and in Him all things consist.
And He is the head of the body, the church, who is
the beginning, the firstborn from the dead, that in all
things He may have the preeminence. For it pleased
the Father that in Him all the fullness should dwell,
and by Him to reconcile all things to Himself, by
Him, whether things on earth or things in heaven,
having made peace through the blood of His cross.
(Colossians 1:16–20)

The Christian is to become like Jesus Christ. This means that
we must have His mind, think as He does, and live to please and
glorify the Father in heaven as He does. The Holy Spirit is present
in the lives of all believers. He empowers us to develop Christlike
characteristics through the Fruit of the Spirit (Galatians 5:22–23).
This means we are to have the mindset that characterized the Son
of God (Philippians 2:5–11).

Let this mind be in you, which was also in Christ
Jesus: who, being in the form of God, thought it not
robbery to be equal with God: but made himself
of no reputation, and took upon him the form of
a servant, and was made in the likeness of men:
and being found in fashion as a man, he humbled
himself, and became obedient unto death, even the
death of the cross. Wherefore God also hath highly
exalted him and given him a name which is above
every name: that at the name of Jesus every knee

should bow, of things in heaven, and things in earth, and things under the earth; and that every tongue should confess that Jesus Christ is Lord, to the glory of God the Father. (Philippians 3:5–11)

The Holy Spirit

The Comforter, or the Holy Spirit, was sent to guide all who believe in Christ and give them the divine power and grace needed to walk the Christian life. The operations of salvation proceed from the Father, through the mediation of the Son, and achieved through the power of the Holy Spirit. This produces spiritual growth or spiritual maturity. Spiritual growth is matured by using the Word of God in the power of the Spirit.

The secret of effectual living is knowing the power of the Word of God through the effectual work of the Holy Spirit. The parable of the sower (Matthew 13:3–23) gives us an understanding of how the seed is sown in our hearts. Just like seed, when the Word of God is spoken, it is scattered upon various kinds of ground. The ground represents the heart. The seed that is sown in fertile soil grows and develops to maturity. This fertile soil represents the person who hears the good news about Jesus Christ and fully comprehends its implications, importance, and meaning. This causes the heart (or inner person) to be convicted, causing a change of conduct and the bearing of spiritual fruit.

It is important that the inner person be "renewed day by day" (2 Corinthians 4:16) through the power of the Word of God and the anointing of the Holy Spirit. A review and role of the Holy Spirit as God is revealed in the following scriptures.

Howbeit when he, the Spirit of truth, is come, he will guide you into all truth: for he shall not speak of himself;

but whatsoever he shall hear, that shall he speak: and he will shew you things to come. (John 16:13)

"But the Helper, the Holy Spirit, whom the Father will send in My name, He will teach you all things, and bring to your remembrance all things that I said to you." (John 14:26)

The Names, Attributes, and Characteristics of God

The names of God are important to us because from them we learn of His awesomeness, supremacy, power, capability, character, and attributes. Scripture not only reveals the nature of God but also helps us to understand His character and behavior. This knowledge is formed when one understands the scope of His ability and power. We will gain an insight into who God is through a study of names, character, and attributes. This account is small and limited regarding the many names, characteristics, and attributes of God.

The Names of God

Having an intimate knowledge of who God is gives us confidence in Him as the source of our life and existence. Scripture not only reveals the personality of God but also helps us understand His nature. A few of them are reviewed in this chapter.

JEHOVAH YAHWEH—Lord, Jehovah—The Omnipotent God

And God spake unto Moses, and said unto him, I am the LORD: And I appeared unto Abraham, unto

> Isaac, and unto Jacob, by the name of God Almighty,
> but by my name JEHOVAH was I not known to
> them. (Exodus 6:2–3)

Jehovah or Yahweh is the covenant name of God. "The self-existent one," "I am who I am," or "I will be who I will be," as revealed to Moses at the burning bush (Exodus 6:2–3). They both imply the same God alone is. He does not depend on anything else. Jehovah is the highest over all the earth. The psalmist David proclaimed, "O LORD our Lord, how excellent is thy name in all the earth!" (Psalm 8:1). We run to Him in the times of trouble. Acts 17:28 declares, "For in him we live, and move, and have our being."

JEHOVAH ADONAI—My Lord and Master

> The LORD said unto my Lord, Sit thou at my right
> hand, until I make thine enemies thy footstool.
> (Psalm 110:1)

> Therefore let all the house of Israel know assuredly,
> that God hath made the same Jesus, whom ye have
> crucified, both Lord and Christ. (Acts 2:36)

Adonai means "master" or "Lord" when referring to God. It speaks of a relationship—our relationship to God. The name Adonai challenges us to live a life that is in obedience to the call and will of God. The full meaning of Adonai is "master" or "sovereign ruler" or "Lord." We are not our own; we belong to God.

Adonai refers to God's ownership of man. He gives a plan and a purpose for each of us and gives us the ability to accomplish those purposes. It is up to us to conform to His plan or will. We must live lives that are in obedience to the calling of God. For Jesus said,

"But why do you call Me 'Lord, Lord'" (ADONAI) and do not do the things which I say?" (Luke 6:46 NKJV).

El SHADDAI—God Almighty, All-Sufficient One

> And when Abram was ninety years old and nine, the Lord appeared to Abram, and said unto him, I am the Almighty God; walk before me, and be thou perfect. And I will make my covenant between me and thee, and will multiply thee exceedingly. (Genesis 17:1–2)

> And God Almighty bless thee, and make thee fruitful, and multiply thee, that thou mayest be a multitude of people. (Genesis 28:3)

El Shaddai means the Almighty, all-sufficient God. The word El means "strength, might, and power." God is our sufficiency. His unlimited might, power, and strength can meet our every need. He is both our strength and our life sustainer. We have no need beyond what He gives us. This refers to God completely nourishing, satisfying, and supplying His people with all their needs as a mother would her child.

JEHOVAH ELOHIM—Lord God Sovereign, Mighty Creator

> In the beginning God created the heaven and the earth. (Genesis 1:1)

> These are the generations of the heavens and of the earth when they were created, in the day that the LORD God made the earth and the heavens. (Genesis 2:4)

The verses show the full power of God as the creator of heaven and earth. Prominently, we see the work of the Holy Spirit in the creation of heaven and earth. The Word confirmed the plurality of Father, Son, and the Holy Spirit as creators of heaven and earth in Genesis chapter 1, verse 26, when he said, "Let us make man in our image, after our likeness." Further, John 1:1–3 clarifies the existence of our Lord Jesus as Elohim, Creator of heaven and earth:

> In the beginning was the Word, and the Word was with God, and the Word was God. The same was in the beginning with God. All things were made by him; and without him was not anything made that was made.

JEHOVAH ELYON—*Lord Most High or the Most High God*

> And he blessed him, and said, Blessed be Abram of the most high God, possessor of heaven and earth: And blessed be the most high God, which hath delivered thine enemies into thy hand. And he gave him tithes of all. (Genesis 14:19–20)

Abraham (also known as Abram) understood and knew what it meant to serve the Most High God. With a total of 318 household servants, Abram fought against five groups of enemy kings and defeated them. He was aware that the Lord Most High God was more powerful than all of the enemy kings and would help him win the battle. As Abram returned from the battle, he met the king of Sodom (Genesis 14:21). He had recovered all the goods and was bringing back his nephew, Lot, and his possessions, together with the women and the other people. The king of Sodom met Abram on the way home from battle and offered to give him all the valuables in exchange for the people. However, Abram refused because he feared the Lord. Significantly, he knew that the victory belonged to the Lord Most High.

JEHOVAH-MEPHALTI, the Lord, My Deliverer

> The LORD is my rock, and my fortress, and my deliverer; my God, my strength, in whom I will trust; my buckler, and the horn of my salvation, and my high tower. (Psalm 18:2)

> Mine eyes are ever toward the LORD; for he shall pluck my feet out of the net. (Psalm 25:15)

The psalmist understood the protective power of the Lord as Jehovah-Mephalti and proclaimed him as "The Lord, My Deliver." Why do we need a deliverer? The Bible states that the "adversary the devil, as a roaring lion, walks about, seeking whom he may devour" (1 Peter 5:8b).

The Lord God is the only one who can deliver us from the hands of the enemy. This deliverance is steadfast, unmovable, and victorious. His strength becomes our rock and fortress. If we keep our eyes fixed on Jehovah-Mephalti, we will gain strength and protection from Him.

JEHOVAH-MA'OZ, the Lord, My Strength, My Fortress

> O LORD, my strength, and my fortress, and my refuge in the day of affliction, the nations shall come unto you from the ends of the earth. (Jeremiah 16:19)

Jeremiah declared his faith in God as he referred to Him in his statement, "O Lord, my strength and my fortress." God had promised that He would restore His people to their land and encouraged him to bear the affliction of the time and hope patiently for the promise of God to come to pass. With that patience, he regained strength to live in the present, for he knew that God was his strength. God's strength provides a refuge in a time of need. He is our shelter and protection.

Jesus Christ came to deliver us from the captivity of Satan, sickness, sin, and afflictions. We know Him as the strength of His people and our refuge in time of trouble. This protection covers all levels of protection. God works as a shield, fortress, protection, shadow, and shelter in the times of need. This does not mean that we will not have physical hardships, tests, and trials. They are meant to toughen us spiritually. The consequences of faith in God strengthen us and guarantee our constant protection from God. Our faith will always be challenged. The Lord is our protection. Always keep in mind that our strength does not come from ourselves but from the Lord. Importantly, when you go through trials, remember that the Holy Spirit lives in you and supplies the power you need to be an overcomer.

JEHOVAH-HOSHE'AH, the Lord Saves, or the Lord My Savior

> Save, Lord: let the king hear us when we call. (Psalm 20:9)

Salvation belongs to those who trust in the Lord. Verse 7 of Psalm 20 declares, "Some trust in chariots, and some in horses: but we will remember the name of the Lord our God." Human and natural means cannot save us. The mighty strength and power of strong horses and manufactured devices cannot secure permanent salvation. Only the King of kings and Lord of lords, the Savior who died for us, can bring us into full victory over the battles and circumstances of life. Only faith and assurance in the resurrection power of the blood of Jesus Christ can save our souls. He is the assurance that we will arise from the dead and sing His praises in heaven.

EL EMUNAH—*The Faithful God*

> Know therefore that the LORD thy God, he is God, the faithful God, which keepeth covenant and mercy with them that love him and keep his commandments to a thousand generations. (Deuteronomy 7:9)

God is faithful and just. He fulfills all His promises to those who love Him and keep His commandments. Prominently, He is bound to us by His eternal blood covenant. The covenant of God is a blood covenant that was sealed with the blood of Jesus Christ and backed up by faithful God Himself.

God loves us. We are a special people to Him. He opens to us the doors to His blessing. Additionally, He gives us the wisdom, knowledge, understanding, as well as the resources to live in His love and keep His commandments. The covenant makes us partakers of God's character.

JEHOVAH JIREH—*The Lord Will Provide*

> So Abraham called that place "The Lord will provide;" as it is said to this day, "On the mount of the Lord it shall be provided." (Genesis 22:14)

Abraham uses the name Jehovah Jireh to name the place on Mount Moriah. He memorialized the sacrifice of Isaac by the Lord substituting a ram for his son. This substitution shows the faithfulness of God to keep His promises and to help us understand that all things work out for our good when God is our helper (Romans 8:28).

JEHOVAH RAPHA—The Lord Our Healer, the God Who Heals

> He heals the brokenhearted, and binds up their wounds. (Psalm 147:3)

Rapha means "to restore," "to heal," or "to make healthful" in Hebrew. Jehovah God is the Great Physician who heals the physical and emotional needs of His people. He has the power to heal every area of our being. He also pardons our iniquities.

JEHOVAH NISSI—The Lord Is My Banner

> And Moses built an altar and called it, "The Lord is my banner. (Exodus 17:15)

The Lord as Jehovah Nissi is the protector of God's children. Moses honored the work of the Lord by building an altar named after Jehovah-Nissi (the Lord our Banner). When the enemy comes to prevail against the people of God, "The Spirit of the Lord will lift up a standard against him" (Isaiah 59:19b).

JEHOVAH SHALOM—The Lord Is Peace

> Then Gideon built an altar there to the Lord, and called it, The Lord is peace. (Judges 6:24)

Judges 6:24 is the only time Jehovah Shalom appears in the Bible. The Lord provided peace for Gideon, a judge from the Old Testament, who, with only three hundred faithful Israelites, defeated a Midianite army of 135,000 soldiers. The angel of the Lord spoke the following words to Gideon the night before the battle: "Peace be with you; do not fear, you shall not die" (Judges 6:23). Jesus said, "Peace I leave with you; my peace I give to you. I do not give to you as the world gives. Do not let your hearts be troubled, and do not let them be afraid" (John 14:27). The Lord is our peace in all our encounters and circumstances.

The Characteristics of God

God does not derive His life or existence from anything or anyone outside of Himself. That is because He is the source of all being and life. Philosophically speaking, everything that comes into being must have a cause. However, God never came into existence and therefore does not require a cause. He has always existed. He is not bound or contained by time or space but goes beyond both. Jesus has always existed as God the Son. He was there in the beginning of creation with God the Father and the Holy Spirit. He came to earth in the form of man to redeem humankind back to God the Father. Scripture gives us a direct insight into His divinity.

> But will God indeed dwell on the earth? behold, the heaven and heaven of heavens cannot contain thee; how much less this house that I have builded. (1 Kings 8:27)

> But, beloved, be not ignorant of this one thing, that one day is with the Lord as a thousand years, and a thousand years as one day. (2 Peter 3:8)

Innate Characteristics of God

In addition to His names, God gives us a direct insight into His deity when He reveals His divine characteristics and attributes. The terms *characteristics* and *attributes* are often used interchangeably. However, there is a difference between the two. God does not share His innate traits with anyone. Characteristics fall in this category. They are traits that are intrinsic and specific to God. No one else has them, and they cannot be found anywhere else. These characteristics include His omnipresence, omniscience, omnipotence, immutability, eternality, and triune nature.

God Is Omnipresent

> Where can I go from your Spirit? Where can I flee from your presence? If I go up to the heavens, you are there; if I make my bed in the depths, you are there. If I rise on the wings of the dawn, if I settle on the far side of the sea, even there your hand will guide me, your right hand will hold me fast. (Psalm 139:7–10)

> Am I a God at hand, saith the Lord, and not a God afar off? Can any hide himself in secret places that I shall not see him? saith the Lord. Do not I fill heaven and earth? saith the Lord. (Jeremiah 23:23–24)

The term *omnipresence* means "everywhere" and "present." God is present everywhere at the same time. He is an everlasting, eternal, omnipotent, and omnipresent God who is always at all places. He is an all-powerful God who has knowledge of all things because He created everything. There is no limit to His knowledge, nor is there a limit to His presence and ability.

God Is Omniscient

> Then hear thou in heaven thy dwelling place, and forgive, and do, and give to every man according to his ways, whose heart thou knowest; (for thou, even thou only, knowest the hearts of all the children of men. (1 Kings 8:39)

> The Lord looketh from heaven; he beholdeth all the sons of men. From the place of his habitation he looketh upon all the inhabitants of the earth. He fashioneth their hearts alike; he considereth all their works. (Psalm 33:13–15)

God is sovereign and self-sufficient. He is unlimited in wisdom and knowledge because He is the source of wisdom and knowledge. He knows all things. Nothing can be hidden from Him. Significantly, He knows each of us and is acquainted with our ways because He has knowledge of our actions and thoughts. This knowledge extends to small as well as to great affairs (Matthew 6:8, 32; 10:30), to the hidden heart and mind of man as well as to that which is open and manifested. Importantly, He listens to us when we pray.

God Is Omnipotent

> And God said, "Let there be light," and there was light. (Genesis 1:3)

> By the word of the LORD were the heavens made,
> their starry host by the breath of his mouth. He
> gathers the waters of the sea into jars; he puts the
> deep into storehouses. Let all the earth fear the
> LORD; let all the people of the world revere him.
> For he spoke, and it came to be; he commanded, and
> it stood firm. (Psalm 33:6–9)

God is all-powerful and all-knowing and has ultimate authority over all things and all creatures. His power is absolute. His power is fixed, exclusive, and unconditional. Uniquely, He is all-powerful and limitless in authority and ability. As we view His works of creation, we see them declaring not only His mighty power but also His infinite wisdom. In effect, His understanding and knowledge supersede man's comprehension.

God Is Immutable

> Of old hast thou laid the foundation of the earth:
> and the heavens are the work of thy hands. They
> shall perish, but thou shalt endure: yea, all of them
> shall wax old like a garment; as a vesture shalt thou
> change them, and they shall be changed: But thou
> art the same, and thy years shall have no end. (Psalm
> 102:25–27)

> For the gifts and calling of God are without
> repentance. (Romans 11:29)

Immutability refers to the unchangeableness of God. God is unchangeable. He is the one Creator of all things and weighs all things by His standards. He is perfect and always remains the same.

This means that there is no change in His attributes, His will, or His purpose. The characteristic is finite and makes Him distinctly God. He is eternal and self-sustaining. He cannot go out of existence and will always remain as He is. Immutability also signifies that His love never changes; His grace does not change; and His will can't change. His entire nature is unchangeable.

God Is Eternal

> The eternal God is thy refuge, and underneath are the everlasting arms: and he shall thrust out the enemy from before thee; and shall say, Destroy them. (Deuteronomy 33:27)

> Lord, thou hast been our dwelling place in all generations. Before the mountains were brought forth, or ever thou hadst formed the earth and the world, even from everlasting to everlasting, thou art God. (Psalm 90:1–2)

The Lord God exists from everlasting to everlasting and exists as the "I am" God. He was here before heaven and earth were created. The entire first chapter of Genesis explains His works of creation and gives further details on how He created the plants and animals on the earth. He then created man.

God Is Triune

> Who being the brightness of his glory, and the express image of his person, and upholding all things by the word of his power, when he had by himself purged

our sins, sat down on the right hand of the Majesty on high. (Hebrews 1:3)

And Jesus, when he was baptized, went up straightway out of the water: and, lo, the heavens were opened unto him, and he saw the Spirit of God descending like a dove, and lighting upon him: And lo a voice from heaven, saying, This is my beloved Son, in whom I am well pleased. (Matthew 3:16–17)

The Lord is one God who has manifested Himself in three divine persons: Father, Son, and Holy Spirit. God the Father refers to the first person in the Trinity. He is reverenced as the Father of redeemed and saved people. Jesus taught us to pray to the "Father" (Matthew 6:9, 14, 26). The Bible reveals God as "the God and Father of the Lord Jesus" (2 Corinthians 11:31). Jesus Christ, or the "Son," was the fullness of the Godhead bodily, "for in him dwelleth all the fulness of the Godhead bodily" (Colossians 2:9). The Comforter, or the Holy Spirit, was sent to guide all who believe in Christ and give them the divine power and grace needed to walk the Christian life.

Attributes of God

Because man is made in God's image, many of God's qualities and traits can be transferred to man. These are His attributes. Attributes are the shared qualities of God that can be transferred to man. Scripture (2 Peter 3:18) says we grow in grace and in the knowledge of Christ. Salvation is by grace. The grace of God makes the righteousness of God a part of man's nature. Man is saved by grace through faith (Ephesians 2:8–9). Faith comes by having a knowledge of God's Word.

The Word sanctifies and causes spiritual maturity. This sanctification process provides the attribute of God that enables us to break free of our sinful nature and become more like Him. As we grow in Christ and are transformed by the work of the Holy Spirit in us (Romans 12:1–2; 2 Corinthians 3:18), His love, goodness, holiness, compassion, and other godly attributes become manifest in our lifestyle and conduct.

God Is Holy

> "For I am the Lord your God: ye shall therefore sanctify yourselves, and ye shall be holy; for I am holy." (Leviticus 11:44)

> The Lord is righteous in all his ways, and holy in all his works. (Psalm 145:17)

God is infinitely holy. He is pure and undefiled. Holiness is an essential character of God and describes His essence, nature, and perfection. Fundamentally, He is righteous, blameless, and perfect. The word *perfect* is translated as "finished," "whole," or "complete" in the Old Testament. God never sins, nor finds the need to repent of sin. As for God, his way is "perfect" (Psalm18:30). The law of God is perfect (Psalm 19:7). Jesus admonished us in the New Testament to be perfect as our heavenly Father is perfect (Matthew 19:21).

God Is Good

> Praise ye the Lord. O give thanks unto the Lord; for He is good: for His mercy endureth forever. (Psalm 106:1)

> That ye may be the children of your Father which is
> in heaven: for He maketh His sun to rise on the evil
> and on the good, and sendeth rain on the just and
> on the unjust. (Matthew 5:45)

All that God originally created was good, an extension of His own nature. He continues to be good to His creation by sustaining it on behalf of all His creatures. He even provides for the ungodly. In addition to being good, the goodness of the Lord is an attribute of all believers. He gives good gifts to all (James 1:17) and provides all with the Fruit of the Holy Spirit (Galatians 5:22, 2).

God Is Love

> For God so loved the world, that he gave his only
> Son, that whoever believes in him should not perish
> but have eternal life. (John 3:16)

> But God shows his love for us in that while we were
> still sinners, Christ died for us. (Romans 5:8)

God's love is a selfless love that embraces the entire world. The chief expression of that love was His sending His only Son, Jesus, to die for sinners. In addition, God has a special family love for those who through Jesus are reconciled to Him.

God Is a Spirit

> God is a Spirit and they that worship Him must
> worship Him in spirit and in truth. (John 4:24)

> Now the Lord is that Spirit: and where the Spirit of
> the Lord is, there is liberty. (2 Corinthians 4:17)

God is a spirit. He is not only living, but He is personal and accessible and infinitely more real than anything in the universe. He reveals Himself to us as Father, Son, and Holy Spirit and is the one, eternal, powerful, and absolute God who created all for worship and fellowship. The heavens and earth cannot hold God; they are contained by Him. His Spirit invades the whole universe because He is the Creator and preserver of the universe and everything in it.

God Is to Be Blessed

> Blessed be the God and Father of our Lord Jesus Christ, which according to His abundant mercy hath begotten us again unto a lively hope by the resurrection of Jesus Christ from the dead to an inheritance incorruptible, and undefiled, and that fadeth not away, reserved in heaven for you. (1 Peter 1:3–4)

> Bless the Lord, O my soul; and all that is within me, bless his holy name! Bless the Lord, O my soul, and forget not all his benefits: Who forgives all your iniquities, who heals all your diseases, Who redeems your life from destruction, who crowns you with loving kindness and tender mercies, Who satisfies your mouth with good things, so that your youth is renewed like the eagle's. (Psalm 103:1–5)

The blessedness of God refers to His inexpressible perfection, the sum of all His identifying parts. Bless the Lord "O my soul" describes the comprehensiveness of blessing the Lord. The Lord is to be adored, worshipped, and praised for His goodness, salvation, and love. Therefore, to bless God is to exalt Him above all.

God Is Truth

> God is not a man, that He should lie; neither the son of man, that He should repent: hath He. (Numbers 23:19)

> Jesus said to him, "I am the way, and the truth, and the life. No one comes to the Father except through me." (John 14:6 ESV)

Jesus called Himself "the Truth," and the Holy Spirit is known as the "Spirit of Truth." Because God is entirely trustworthy and true in all He says and does, it is a confirmation of truth. His Word is truth because it is "impossible for Him to lie." God is patient and slow to anger. God first expressed this characteristic in the Garden of Eden after Adam and Eve's sin, when He did not destroy humanity, as He had a right to do. God was also patient in the days of Noah, while the ark was being built. And God is still patient with the sinful human race; He does not presently judge to destroy the world because He is patiently giving everyone the opportunity to repent and be saved through the truth of His Word.

God Is Compassionate

> But thou. O Lord, art a God full of compassion, and gracious, longsuffering, and plenteous in mercy and truth. (Psalm 86:15)

> The Spirit of the Lord is upon me, because He hath anointed me to preach the gospel the poor; He hath sent me to heal the broken hearted, to preach deliverance to the captive, and recovering of sight to the blind, to set at liberty them that are bruised, to preach the acceptable year of the Lord. (Luke 4:18–19)

To be compassionate means to feel sorrow for someone else's suffering, with a desire to help. Out of His compassion for humanity, God provided forgiveness and salvation; likewise, Jesus, the Son of God, showed compassion for the crowds when He preached the gospel to the poor, proclaimed freedom for the prisoners, gave sight to the blind, and released the oppressed.

God Is Merciful

> Blessed be God, even the Father of our Lord Jesus Christ, the Father of mercies and the God of all comfort. (1 Corinthians 1:3)

> I will sing of the mercies of the Lord forever: with my mouth will I make known thy faithfulness to all generations. For I have said, Mercy shall be build up for ever: thy faithfulness shalt thou establish in the very heavens. (Psalm 89:1–2)

The Lord does not cut off and destroy humanity as our sins deserve, but He offers forgiveness as a free gift to be received through faith in Jesus Christ. He is free in His goodness to those who have neither deserved nor merited in any manner His goodness. God gives out of love, not out of obligation or necessity. To those in misery and need, God displays His love through a tender, personal, and eternal interest. For this reason, He is addressed as "the Father of mercies and God of all comfort."

The Lord Is All-Wise

> If any of you lacks wisdom, he should ask God, who gives generously to all without finding fault, and it will be given to him. (James 1:5)

> O Lord, how manifold are thy works! in wisdom hast thou made them all: the earth is full of thy riches. (Psalm 104:24)

The wisdom of God is seen through His many works of creation. *Vine's Expository Dictionary of New Testament* [7] defines wisdom as an attribute of God. Wisdom is intimately related to the divine knowledge, manifesting itself in the selection of proper ends with the proper means for their accomplishment. Therefore, not only the world of nature but especially the economy of redemption is a manifestation of divine wisdom.

PEACE AND QUIETNESS

Word Seed: "Mercy and truth are met together; righteousness and peace have kissed each other. Truth shall spring out of the earth; and righteousness shall look down from heaven" (Psalm 85:10 KJV).

The Seed of the Word

Another term that can be used for mercy is loving-kindness. Mercy is love that is kind when the situation says it should not be. Jesus fulfilled this scripture when He died to reconcile the world to God. Because of His love, mercy, death, and resurrection, the believer has eternal life (Romans 10:9–11). The believer is declared righteous in Jesus not because of who he is or what he has done but because of who Jesus is (Ephesians 2:8–9). The joining of righteousness and peace brings peace with God and forgiveness of sins (Romans 5:1).

The Action of the Word

The Lord is good. He is not only good but also merciful and faithful (Psalm 100:5). There is no end to His mercy and faithfulness. His loving-kindness embraces the life of every person and touches every situation. He is good. His mercy and truth extend throughout eternity. He is steadfast. His Word will not return to Him void; neither will His promises come to naught. Every generation that has ever lived on earth has witnessed his faithfulness. His Word has endured throughout all generations, and His goodness reaches to the sky. All of His promises have been or will be met. He is our all and all.

The Persistence of the Word

God is our refuge and strength, always ready to help in times of trouble. Peace represents a state of calmness or quietness of spirit that goes beyond any circumstance. The Lord is our refuge and our strength, meaning He is our peace. When we develop a lifestyle of making the Lord our refuge, we begin to live in His peace. While life situations change and conditions are transformed or adjusted on earth, God's Word is always there to bring up those who are fearful, live in doubt, or have no hope. The Lord is the same as He has always been. His peace passes all human knowledge and understanding (Philippians 4:7).

What Is This Word Saying to You?

RECEIVING WISDOM

Word Seed: "For those who find me find life and receive favor from the Lord" (Proverbs 8:35).

The Seed of the Word

Wisdom comes directly from God and is revealed in His Word. It especially centers in the knowledge of Christ. James 1:5 asserts that individuals who feel they lack wisdom should ask God to give them wisdom. He further declares that the Lord would not only answer their requests, but He would be generous in giving them wisdom. The term *favor* is usually associated with grace in the Bible. Grace is given to all who would accept Christ as Savior. They are declared righteous and accepted as sons of God and joint heirs with Jesus Christ (Romans 8:17).

The Action of the Word

The knowledge of the Lord brings wisdom. Wisdom is knowledge applied. Reading the Bible brings the knowledge of God, and meditating upon that knowledge brings wisdom. The Holy Spirit works with our spirit to produce revelation knowledge. Reading the Word of God and meditating on what the Lord is saying renews the mind and reveals God's truths (Romans 12:2; 2 Timothy 2:15; John 8:32). Everyone experiences fear, doubt, or unbelief. However, those who are wise and obey the commands of God will receive favor from God. Favor from God means He accepts or gives His seal of approval. Furthermore, when our thoughts align with God's thoughts, we become wise, our minds become renewed, and we gain His unmerited grace and favor.

The Persistence of the Word

Having wisdom is like having a garden that is fed and watered by the Word of God (Isaiah 58:11). Everyone who drinks from God's Word receives an overflow of the water of life. Wisdom is more than receiving information; it is receiving knowledge of the characteristics, will, and favor of God. It is living in relationship with a living God who calls one to Himself and allows him to feed from His table. That intimate relationship comes from an overflowing of the favor of God. All of God's promises become revealed when the mind is renewed.

What Is This Word Saying to You?

GREAT ARE THE WORKS OF THE LORD

Word Seed: "The fear of the LORD is the beginning of wisdom; A good understanding have all those who do His commandments. His praise endures forever" (Psalm 111:10).

The Seed of the Word

The fear of the Lord is essential for obtaining godly wisdom and a good understanding of who God is. This translates into a life of holiness, reverence, righteousness, and obedience to God's will. So what is the fear of the Lord? The fear of the Lord is giving Him complete reverence as the Almighty God, who is worthy to be worshipped, honored, exalted, and obeyed. Fear includes being obedient to His commands, lordship, and authority.

The Action of the Word

Psalm 111 is an excellent scripture to use to meditate on, praise, and give thanks to the Lord for His goodness. It starts with hallelujah. Hallelujah is the highest praise one can give. Fearing the Lord comes from having a knowledge of the need to praise Him for His blessings and wonderful deeds. One is reminded of His goodness and wonderful acts in the events of the Bible. We find His goodness revealed in the events of the Exodus from Egypt, the rescue of Daniel when he was in the lion's den, the healing of the ten lepers, and Christ's death on the cross. Understanding Him causes one to be in awe of His glory and power. This is declared in Exodus 34:6 when Moses praised him for His mercy and steadfast love. The Lord is a deliverer. His actions in the wilderness and the crossing of the Red Sea show His supremacy and authority over all of nature. Holy and awesome are His works. Fear of the Lord can be equated with love. Entering into a relationship with the Lord comes when one understands and respects His authority.

The Persistence of the Word

Fearing the Lord helps to keep a proper perspective of who we are in relation to His sovereignty and motivates us to be more like Him. The psalm causes us to praise the Lord with urgency and rejoice in our hearts, for He is worthy to be praised! Importantly, godly fear helps to focus on the consequences of disobedience.

What Is This Word Saying to You?

THE MEANING AND IMPORTANCE OF HOLY COMMUNION / THE LORD'S SUPPER

Word Seed: "The cup of blessing which we bless, is it not the communion of the blood of Christ? The bread which we break, is it not the communion of the body of Christ? For we, though many, are one bread and one body; for we all partake of that one bread" (1 Corinthians 10:16–17).

The Seed of the Word

Jesus Christ is the life source of the believer. God the Father is the life source of Jesus. God took all our sicknesses and diseases and put them on Jesus's originally perfect and healthy body when He died on the cross of Calvary. The purpose was so that we would walk in divine health and be freed from sin. Sharing Communion unites all believers from all ages in the death and resurrection of Christ. When we take Communion, we are proclaiming to the world both the seen and the unseen, the Lord's death, and the price He paid for our salvation. We are not simply remembering Jesus. We are coming to the table to eat with Him and to be spiritually nourished by Him.

The Action of the Word

"And he said unto them, With desire I have desired to eat this Passover with you before I suffer: And he took bread, and gave thanks, and break it, and gave unto them, saying, This is my body which is given for you: this do in remembrance of me. Likewise, also the cup after supper, saying, This cup is the new testament in my blood, which is shed for you" (Luke 22:15, 19–20). Jesus was eating the Passover meal with His disciples the night before His crucifixion when He spoke those words. The Passover occurred during one of the plagues mentioned in the twelfth chapter of the book of Exodus, when God killed every Egyptian firstborn male but passed over the homes of the Israelites who put lamb's blood on their doorposts. The Feast of the Passover commemorates this deliverance and the salvation of the Israelites from the Egyptians (Exodus 12:27). A male lamb without blemish was slaughtered and eaten at the feast. God sacrificed His only begotten Son as "a lamb without blemish" (1 Peter 1:19), to bring salvation to all who accept Jesus Christ as Lord and Savior.

The Persistence of the Word

Jesus Christ is the bread of life, the hidden manna sent from heaven. He gave His life as a ransom for the sins of mankind. The unleavened bread taken during Communion represents His sinless body. The cup symbolizes his life-giving blood, which was shed as an offering to pay the price for our sins.

What Is This Word Saying to You?

THE POWER OF THE BLOOD OF CHRIST

Word Seed: "The next day he saw Jesus coming toward him and said, 'Behold, the Lamb of God, who takes away the sin of the world'" (John 1:29).

The Seed of the Word

When John the Baptist saw Jesus approaching before he baptized Him, he cried out, "Look, the Lamb of God, who takes away the sin of the world" (John 1:29). During the time of the plagues, as recorded in the book of Exodus, God told Moses to tell the Israelites to paint lamb's blood on their doorposts. This way, the angel would know that Jewish people lived there. The angel would pass over that house and not kill the firstborn child. This initiated Passover. Jesus was crucified as our Passover Lamb, and He rose as our resurrected Lord and Savior. Without the shedding of the blood of Jesus and His substitutionary death, we would have no hope of salvation. When we take part in Holy Communion, we are "proclaiming the Lord's death till He comes" (1 Corinthians 11:26).

The Action of the Word

The shedding of blood at the cross of Calvary is the basis for our victory over the enemy of our souls. There is healing in the bread we take in Holy Communion. It is symbolic of the body of Christ, which was broken for us. His blood was shed to establish a new covenant, forgive sins, redeem believers, and cleanse and sanctify us from sin and shame. He took on all sin, iniquity, rebellion, disease, grief, and shame. "And they overcame him by the blood of the Lamb, and by the word of their testimony; and they loved not their lives unto the death" (Revelation 12:11).

The Persistence of the Word

Jesus won a victory on the cross. He overcame Satan, sin, and death by His blood. When we celebrate the Lord's Supper, we should be reminded that He overcame the enemy of our soul completely when He shed His blood for our sins. The blood of the New Covenant is that Jesus Christ paid not only for our sins but for the full provision for every need in our lives. All we need to do is believe that and enforce that victory over our lives by aligning our lives and our words with God's Word.

What Is This Word Saying to You?

HALLELUJAH, SALVATION, HONOR, AND POWER TO OUR GOD!

Word Seed: "Alleluia; Salvation, and glory, and honor, and power, unto the Lord our God" (Revelation 19:1b).

The Seed of the Word

God deserves glory, honor, and power because He is the sovereign Lord who created and rules the universe (Genesis 1:1). We were created to worship Him. Hallelujah is the highest form of praise. It is a declaration of confidence in the Almighty God, who saved and delivers. Salvation refers to deliverance of God's people from Satan, sin, and hell. Most significant, salvation is a manifestation of God's omnipotence, mercy, love, and holiness. All glory belongs to Him. Glory is the manifested presence of God. However, glory is more than just His presence; it is His power, the power that resurrects, delivers, overcomes, and transforms lives and situations. Our praises demonstrate the highest regard we have for the Lord. For when we praise Him, we reflect His glory.

The Action of the Word

When we fall to our knees or bow our heads in prayer to the Lord, we usually go over a list of requests and concerns to bring before the Lord. Those concerns are important, and they deserve our time in prayer. But how much of that time do we spend in praise and worship to God? Praise brings us into God's presence and releases the power of God. "God inhabits in the praises of His people" (Psalm 22:3) and should be included in our prayers. "Blessed is the people that know the joyful sound: they shall walk, O LORD, in the light of thy countenance" (Psalm 89:15).

The Persistence of the Word

"Surely God is my salvation; I will trust and not be afraid. The Lord, the Lord himself, is my strength and my defense; he has become my salvation." With joy, you will draw water from the wells of salvation (Isaiah 12:2–3). The joy of the Lord is our strength (Nehemiah 8:10). Joy is a constant gladness that stems from an inner strengthening from the Lord (our salvation). When we delight in the Lord and meditate on His Word day and night, we become like trees planted by streams of living water. These trees bear spiritual fruit that brings blessings to God's kingdom (Psalm 1:3).

What Is This Word Saying to You?

LET US GO OVER TO THE OTHER SIDE

Word Seed: "Jesus said to His Disciples, 'Let us cross over to the other side. And a great windstorm arose, and the waves beat into the boat, so that it was already filling. But He was in the stern, asleep on a pillow. And they awoke Him and said to Him, 'Master, do You not care that we are perishing? Then He arose and rebuked the wind, and said to the sea, 'Peace, be still!' And the wind ceased and there was a great calm" (Mark 4:35–39 NKJV).

The Seed of the Word

Before Jesus spoke to the storm, He spoke to the disciples. He does the same to us today. Before He speaks to the storms that try to invade our lives, He speaks to us, because He wants us to be in position to withstand the storm when it comes. And if He says we are going over, then we are going over! The important thing to know about storms is that they reveal our need to trust God. But we must be in position to hear His voice, and we have to stay anchored in the Lord when the storms come, because His presence brings peace, even in the midst of the storm.

The Action of the Word

After Jesus performed the miracle of feeding over four thousand people with seven small loaves of bread and a few small fish, the Pharisees came to Him and demanded that He give them a sign from heaven. Jesus refused and left. It seems that all that He had already done should have been enough for them (Mark 8:11–13). Jesus cared. But He knew that they had already made up their minds and would not debate with them. A miracle shows God's power and love. It is also a call to faith and should lead to belief.

The Persistence of the Word

Word Seed: After feeding the 5,000, Jesus made His disciples get into the boat and go before Him to the other side. After the disciples left, Jesus prayed. While He prayed, a storm arose in the sea (Matthew 6:22-24). Jesus went to them, walking on the sea. And when the disciples saw Him walking on the sea, they were troubled. But Jesus spoke to them, saying, "Be of good cheer! It is I; do not be afraid. 'And Peter answered Him and said, 'Lord, if it is You, command me to come to You on the water. 'So, He said, 'Come'" (Matthew 14:25–31). When Peter had his eyes on Jesus, he had faith to do the impossible. But he started to sink when he took his eyes off Jesus to focus on the wind and storm. Faith releases the supernatural power of God, but fear will cause you to sink.

What Is This Word Saying to You?

THE HOLY SPIRIT IS OUR SOURCE

Word Seed: "Now we have received, not the spirit of the world, but the spirit which is of God; that we might know the things that are freely given to us of God. Which things also we speak, not in the words which man's wisdom teaches, but which the Holy Ghost teaches; comparing spiritual things with spiritual" (1 Corinthians 2:12–13).

The Seed of the Word

The Holy Spirit sees and knows everything that goes on in our hearts and minds. Nothing is hidden from Him. As the third person of the Godhead, He possesses a complete personality of His own. Significantly, God reveals His Will to us through the Holy Spirit: "But as it is written: 'Eye has not seen, nor ear heard, Nor have entered into the heart of man The things which God has prepared for those who love Him. But God has revealed them to us through His Spirit. For the Spirit searches all things, yes, the deep things of God. For what man knows the things of a man except the spirit of the man which is in him? Even so no one knows the things of God except the Spirit of God'" (1 Corinthians 2:9–11).

The Action of the Word

God reveals His will to us through the Holy Spirit. The Holy Spirit works in our hearts by opening our minds to the mysteries of the truth of God's Word. Then He guides us in the direction that we need to go by giving us a clear view of the meaning of God's Word. Sin offends God and keeps us from living a godly life. Conviction comes before sin happens. When we are confronted with sin and temptation, the Holy Spirit taps on our hearts to remind us of the will of God. It is our responsibility to respond to that conviction. Temptation in itself is not a sin. Jesus was tempted and did not sin. Giving in to temptation is what brings sin.

The Persistence of the Word

No one can follow Christ without the help of the Holy Spirit. To explain it further, the Holy Spirit is to our spiritual lives what God (the Creator) is to the world. Without God, the world would never have come into existence, and without His sustaining power, the world would easily crash out of existence. Equally, without the Spirit of God, Christians would not be able to live by faith. As our Helper, the Holy Spirit comes alongside us in every situation. Our bodies are the temples of the Holy Spirit, and the Holy Spirit helps us live the Christian life.

What Is This Word Saying to You?

ALL THINGS ARE POSSIBLE WITH GOD

Word Seed: "But Jesus beheld them, and said unto them, With men this is impossible; but with God all things are possible" (Matthew 19:26).

The Seed of the Word

God has supreme power over the world and the universe. He has no limitations. But He wants us to know that our faith in Him is what makes the impossible possible. The impossible is not always some big miracle. Sometimes it is God changing us from the inside out. The important thing is that our beliefs must be in alignment with God's will. Jesus knew that He did not have to go to the cross. He also knew that it was possible for God to keep Him from that suffering. Yet He went to the cross anyway, because He knew that it was God's plan from the beginning to send Him to die on the cross for the sins of mankind.

The Action of the Word

God's promises are conditioned upon our following His directions There are consequences for disobedience. Disobedience brings sorrow and hardship. Obedience brings joy and peace, even in the midst of hardship. God is our great provider. He specializes in taking humanly impossible situations and turning them around for His glory. Our responsibility is to wait on Him to lead and guide us through prayer, worship, reading His Word, and having a personal relationship with Him. Setting a goal to obey the Lord makes the impossible possible.

The Persistence of the Word

The Lord looks for those whose hearts (thoughts and feelings) are completely His. When He finds them, "He shows Himself "strong" on their behalf" (2 Chronicles 16:9). The Hebrew word *strong* here means to "take hold of someone, then attach yourself to someone; so as to become their strength." When we are strengthened by the Lord, we receive power and ability to do the supernatural because our ability is in the hands of God. Nothing that He wants to do for us is impossible for Him (Philippians 4:13). That is why we can say, "For Christ's sake, I delight in weaknesses, in insults, in hardships, in persecutions, in difficulties. For when I am weak, then I am strong" (2 Corinthians 12:10).

What Is This Word Saying to You?

THE IMMUTABILITY OF GOD: HE DOES NOT CHANGE

Word Seed: "For I the LORD do not change" (Malachi 3:6).

The Seed of the Word

We live in a world where things are changing rapidly all around us. But God is unchanging. He is unchanging in His attributes, in His perfections, in His plans, and in His will. The will of God is that all be saved and come to repentance (2 Peter 3:9). His attributes are too many to name. We know that the Almighty God is omnipotent (all-powerful), omniscient (all-knowing), and omnipresent (everywhere at the same time). Nothing can be added to Him, and nothing can be taken from him. What He is today He always was and will always be. God is good (Exodus 34:6). He is not only good but is the source of all goodness. His goodness motivates everything that He does. And His promises occur in the context of His love for us, including His Son, Jesus Christ, dying on the cross for our sins.

The Action of the Word

Word Seed: "Thou art the Christ, the Son of the living God. And upon this rock I will build my church; and the gates of hell shall not prevail against it" (Matthew 16:16b, 18b).

Jesus had asked His disciples a question: "Who do men say that I, the Son of Man, am?" Peter spoke up first—"Thou art the Christ, the Son of the living God." Instead of just complimenting Peter for speaking correctly, Jesus Christ made a statement about rocks. He said, Simon Peter replied, "You are the Christ (the Messiah, the Anointed), the Son of the living God." 'Then Jesus answered him, "Blessed [happy, spiritually secure, favored by God] are you, Simon son of Jonah, because flesh and blood (mortal man) did not reveal this to you, but My Father who is in heaven. And I say to you that you are Peter, and on this] rock I will build My church; and the gates of Hades (death) will not overpower it [by preventing the resurrection of the Christ]" (Matthew 16:13–18 AMP).

The Persistence of the Word

The kingdom of God is where the Lord God reigns supremely. When questioned about the "Kingdom of God" in Luke 17, Jesus said, "The Kingdom of God does not come with observation;" meaning it is not an earthly power. The Kingdom of God is the spiritual rule over the hearts and lives of God's people, consisting of righteousness, peace, and joy in the Holy Ghost" (Romans 14:17). The fruit of the Spirit, "love, joy, peace, patience, kindness, goodness, faithfulness, gentleness, and long-suffering" (Galatians 5:22–23), are the results of the work of the Holy Spirit in our hearts.

What Is the Word Saying to You?

THE LIFE-GIVING POWER OF GOD'S WORD

Word Seed: "The LORD said to me, 'You have seen correctly, for I am watching to see that my word is fulfilled" (Jeremiah 1:12 NIV).

The Seed of the Word

Nothing is impossible with respect to any of God's promises. Importantly, "no word from Him shall be without power or fulfillment" (Luke 1:37b AMPC). There is often a gap between seeing a promise of God in His Word and experiencing the fulfillment of that promises. That is because some of the promises in the Bible are conditional. We must meet the conditions of those promises before they are fulfilled in our lives. We must also be aware that God's promises are based on His perfect timing and purposes. For example, the desire to get married is a good one. However, God's slowness in fulfilling that promise may be His way of giving us something better or keeping up from making a terrible mistake.

The Action of the Word

Hebrews 4:12–13 says that God's Word is life giving. It can help people understand their hearts and discern their attitudes. The Lord is an omniscient, omnipresent, and omnipotent God. He is all wise and all-knowing and has a knowledge of everything that happens. Nothing is left unexposed to Him. His Word has power to convert sinners and build up God's people by exposing our sin and pointing to God's grace at the cross. The Word has life; it has producing effects and helps us to see true selves.

The Persistence of the Word

God's Word will never fail. His promises are firm and unfailing. Our unbelief and lack of knowledge can prevent its fulfilment in our lives. All things in life go through seasons. We can see that in nature. The grass begins to wither during the fall season. Additionally, flowers lose their beauty, and tree leaves start wasting awaiting and falling to the ground. The other seasons winter, spring, and summer, have natural occurrences that happen annually. But God does not change. He sits calmly and unmoved, regardless of the changes that occur on earth. His promises are faithful, His warnings are not empty threats, and He offers salvation to all who come to Him in faith.

What Is This Word Saying to You?

GOD IS FAITHFUL

Word Seed: "The LORD is my light and my salvation; Whom shall I fear? The LORD is the strength of my life; Of whom shall I be afraid?" (Psalm 27:1).

The Seed of the Word

Deuteronomy 31:8 assures us, "It is the Lord who goes before you. He will be with you; he will not fail you or forsake you. Do not fear or be dismayed." And we can infer and understand from Psalm 27:1 that the Lord divinely protects us from evil and harm. The Lord is our light. Light always overcomes darkness. And just as light overcomes darkness, God is victorious over evil. Significantly, He is more powerful than the enemy (who represents darkness). The Lord is also our salvation. He is always there to protect and deliver us from danger, diseases, and all catastrophic occurrences. Furthermore, He is faithful. "For in the time of trouble He shall hide me in His pavilion; In the secret place of His Tabernacle, He shall hide me; He shall set me high upon a rock" (verse 5).

The Action of the Word

All have experienced feelings of heartache, distress, and hopelessness. Yet there is always hope because the steadfast love of the Lord never ceases (Lamentations 3:22). This is not just a cliché that sounds spiritual; it is a promise that can change our lives. The Lord, who is the same yesterday, today and forever, has promised never to leave or forsake us (Deuteronomy 31:6).

The Persistence of the Word

The following scripture helps us to understand the world in which we live: "But know this, that in the last days perilous times will come: For men will be lovers of themselves, lovers of money, boasters, proud, blasphemers, disobedient to parents, unthankful, unholy, unloving, unforgiving, slanderers, without self-control, brutal, despisers of good, traitors, headstrong, haughty, lovers of pleasure rather than lovers of God, having a form of godliness but denying its power" (2 Timothy 3:1–5). He expects us to turn to Him in times of need, to be obedient to His Word, and to stand on His promises.

What Is This Word Saying to You?

THE WORK OF THE HOLY SPIRIT

Word Seed: "Whoever believes in me, as the Scriptures said, out of his heart will flow rivers of living water" (John 7:38 NKJV).

The Seed of the Word

Jesus was referring to Ezekiel 47 when he spoke the words of the key scripture. The "rivers of living water" came from a vision that the prophet Ezekiel had when he was in the temple of the Lord. During the vision, he saw a small trickle of water flowing from the altar of the temple. The flow of that water became a stream and then a mighty river. We can read verse 39 of the seventh chapter of John to understand that Jesus was speaking of the Holy Spirit. The Holy Spirit is the stream that takes up permanent residence within our hearts (1 Corinthians 6:9) and changes our lives and behaviors and how we treat others. We need to walk, live, and have our being according to the Holy Spirit. Then we will speak Christ every day and everywhere.

The Action of the Word

Although Jesus Christ was fully God, He drew all His strength from His Father in heaven. He demonstrated how we should live our lives as God's children, drawing all our strength from Him, for "without Him we can do nothing" (John 15:5). Christians have been called to live in the overflow of Christ's supreme and divine love. There is a joyful, victorious, and abundant life in that overflow that is available to the believer that far surpasses natural limitations. It comes through the baptism of the Holy Spirit and a desire to fully live the Spirit-filled life. Jesus is the vine, and we are the branches. We are to abide in Him and allow His Spirit to live His life through us.

The Persistence of the Word

The Holy Spirit confirms God's Word and convicts the heart of sin and the need for salvation. We can't live apart from God's Word. The Spirit also comforts our hearts and minds during times of distress and need. He teaches us to obey God and counsels us when we are weak. The Holy Spirit helps us to know God better by revealing God's Word (thoughts) to believers. This opens their eyes to the hope of salvation and the inheritance they have in Christ.

What Is This Word Saying to You?

THE GOODNESS OF THE LORD

Word Seed: "Oh, how great is Your goodness, Which You have laid up for those who fear You, which You have prepared for those who trust in You" (Psalm 31:19a).

The Seed of the Word

No matter what happens in our lives, we must always have faith that God is working just for us and that He is good. Goodness is the nature and characteristic of who God is. Notably, the Lord God is the source of all goodness. If you want to see the Lord for who He really is, here are some scriptures with good starting points: "Give thanks to the Lord, for He is good" (1 Chronicles 16:34). "Taste and see that the Lord is good" (Psalm 34:8). "Enter His gates with thanksgiving, and His courts with praise! Give thanks to Him and praise His name! For the Lord is good and His love is eternal, and His faithfulness endures to all generations" (Psalm 100:4–5). Those who take refuge in the Lord will be protected and blessed.

The Action of the Word

The Lord God is not only good, but He is also sovereign and has the wisdom, power, and authority to do whatever He chooses. There is no limit to what He can do when answering our prayers because His has the power to go far above and beyond anything we can ask, dream, or even comprehend (Psalm 147:5). We cannot forget how He created a highway in the Red Sea for Moses and the children of Israel. He not only created the highway, but He also provided manna for the three and a half million children of Israel to eat throughout their forty-year journey (Exodus 16:1–36). He also provided a rock for them to drink from during those forty years (Numbers 20:2 13).

Those who take refuge in Him will be protected and blessed. What should we do when we face seemingly impossible situations? We should ask God for His help and then trust in Him. Who would have thought you could get water from a rock?

The Persistence of the Lord

Moses asked the Lord God to show him His glory in Exodus 36. The Hebrew word for *glory* means "heaviness" or "weight" and was used to express the worth of a person. God replied, "I will make all my goodness pass before you" (Exodus 36:18–19a). What is God's glory? What was He saying to Moses? The Lord was telling Moses that His glory was the totality of who He is, including His presence, power, and goodness. Those who take refuge in Him will be protected and blessed.

What Is This Word Saying to You?

THE WORD OF GOD IS ALIVE AND POWERFUL

Word Seed: "For the word of God is living and powerful, and sharper than any two-edged sword, piercing even to the division of soul and spirit, and of joints and marrow, and is a discerner of the thoughts and intents of the heart" (Hebrews 4:12).

The Seed of the Word

The Lord God is omniscient. Nothing is hidden from Him. He is also alive and active, so his Word is alive and active. This means the words in the Bible have the power to convict, speak to us directly, and even transform our lives by cutting deep and entering the depths of our hearts. Hebrews 4:13 says, "Nothing in all creation is hidden from God's sight, Everything is uncovered and laid bare before the eyes of him to whom we must give account." "Therefore, since we have a great high priest who has ascended into heaven, Jesus the Son of God, let us hold firmly to the faith we profess. For we do not have a high priest who is unable to empathize with our weaknesses, but we have one who has been tempted in every way, just as we are—yet he did not sin" (Hebrews 4:14–15).

The Action of the Word

We can teach, reprove, correct, train, and communicate information to the mind, but we cannot speak truth to the heart of a person. Only God can do that. In other words, if the truth reaches the heart, it is because the Holy Spirit brings it about. Therefore, Paul appealed to members of the church in Rome not to be "conformed to this world, but to be transformed by the renewing of your mind" (Romans 12:1–2) through the power of God's Spirit. This takes prayer, reading and meditating on the Word of God, along with spending time with God.

The Persistence of the Word

The Lord is revealed in three persons: God the father, the Son, and the Holy Spirit. The Father gave His Son to die for us. Jesus paid the penalty for our sins, and the Holy Spirit provides spiritual enlightenment to our spirits for us to know the Father and the Lord Jesus. Jesus is expressed as the Word in John 1:1–12: There is power in the Word. Jesus demonstrated that power when He spoke to a fig tree, and it died (Mark 11:22–25). Believers have that same power and authority over the enemy when we say and do what the Word of God says.

What Is This Word Saying to You?

4

THE PLAN OF SALVATION

B EING BORN AGAIN IS REFERRED TO AS SALVATION. SALVATION IS based upon faith in Jesus Christ and the acknowledgment that He is the Son of God. Salvation is the release from the power and dominion of sin. Significantly, it is the grace of God delivering His people from bondage to sin and condemnation, transferring them to the kingdom of His beloved Son (Colossians 1:13) and giving them eternal life. With this comes deliverance from trouble, the devil, or danger.

> For God so loved the world, that He gave His only begotten Son, that whosoever believeth in Him should not perish, but have everlasting life. (John 3:16)

> And she shall bring forth a son, and thou shalt call his name Jesus: for he shall save his people from their sins. (Matthew 1:21)

> Who hath delivered us from the power of darkness, and hath translated us into the kingdom of his dear Son. (Colossians 1:13)

Several referenced sources provide the following definition and information on salvation.

1. *Vine's Expository Dictionary of New Testament*[8] defines salvation (*soteria*) as "the spiritual and eternal deliverance granted immediately by God to those who accept His conditions of repentance and faith in the Lord Jesus, in whom alone it is to be obtained."

2. Arthur W. Pink[9] defines salvation as "the present possession of all true Christians future salvation, the sum of benefits and blessings which the Christians, redeemed from all earthly ills, will enjoy after the visible return of Christ from heaven in the consummated and eternal kingdom of God."

Pink's[10] described salvation as being a progress of developments, beginning with the Lord's promise to provide a Redeemer for man's salvation, and expanding throughout eternity. Each progressive stage is briefly examined and accompanied by a Word Seed.

First, salvation comes by repentance and faith. Scripture shows how "your faith has saved you" (Luke 7:50); affirms that "you are saved by grace" (Ephesians 2:8); and asserts that "according to His mercy He saved us" (Titus 3:5).

> And he said to the woman, Thy faith hath saved thee; go in peace. (Luke 7:50)

> "For it is by grace you have been saved, through faith—and this is not from yourselves, it is the gift of God; not by works, so that no one can boast. (Ephesians 2:8–9 NIV).

Not by works of righteousness which we have done, but according to his mercy he saved us, by the washing of regeneration, and renewing of the Holy Ghost. (Titus 3:5)

Second, salvation is present victory. It is being presently accomplished and not yet completed, "Unto us which are being saved" (1 Corinthians 1:18), "Those who believe to the saving (not 'salvation') of the soul" (Hebrews 10:39).

For the preaching of the cross is to them that perish foolishness; but unto us which are saved it is the power of God. (1 Corinthians 1:18)

But we are not of them who draw back unto perdition; but of them that believe to the saving of the soul. (Hebrews 10:39)

Third, salvation as a future privilege. Jesus was "sent forth to minister for them who shall be heirs of salvation" (Hebrews 1:14); believers are to "receive with meekness the engrafted Word, which is able to save your souls" (James 1:21). Believers are "kept by the power of God through faith unto salvation, ready to be revealed in the last time" (1 Peter 1:5).

Are they not all ministering spirits, sent forth to minister for them who shall be heirs of salvation? (Hebrews 1:14)

Pink[11] summarized salvation by saying, "In Adam all die" (1 Corinthians 15:22), "By the offense of one, judgment came upon all men to condemnation" (Romans 5:18). The result of this is that all are "alienated from the life of God through the ignorance that is in them, because of the blindness of their hearts" (Ephesians 4:18), so that the members of the mystical body of Christ are "by nature the children of wrath, even as others" (Ephesians 2:3:), and hence they are alike in dire need of God's salvation (Pink, 47).

> For as in Adam all die, even so in Christ shall all be made alive. (1 Corinthians 15:22)

> Therefore, as by the offence of one judgment came upon all men to condemnation; even so by the righteousness of one the free gift came upon all men unto justification of life. (Romans 5:18)

> Having the understanding darkened, being alienated from the life of God through the ignorance that is in them, because of the blindness of their heart. (Ephesians 4:18)

> Among whom also we all had our conversation in times past in the lusts of our flesh, fulfilling the desires of the flesh and of the mind; and were by nature the children of wrath, even as others. (Ephesians 2:3)

The Fall of Man

In the beginning, God created the heavens and the earth (Genesis 1:1). God looked upon all He had created and concluded that it was "very good" (Genesis 1:31). His last creation was that of man. God created Adam and Eve in His own image and placed them in the Garden of Eden (Genesis 1:26–27). Adam and Even had complete fellowship with God until, through deception and disobedience, Adam and Eve sinned against Him (Genesis chapters 1–3). Sin entered into the world as a result of their disobedience. That caused all future men and women to have a nature and an impulse toward sin and evil.

Sin

Vine's Expository Dictionary of New Testament[12] defines sin as "a missing of the mark."

Vine's continued by asserting that "sin can be broadly defined as any attitude or action that opposes the character and will of God. Sin is what brings death—that is, separation from God. Sin can be broadly defined as any attitude or action that opposes the character and will of God."

> We were all born in sin and shaped in iniquity. (Psalm 51:5)

Jesus Came to Save Mankind from Sin and Restore to God

Matthew 1:21 prophesied that Jesus "will save his people from their sins." Sin is what separates mankind from God. Jesus is the Word that was made flesh in order to redeem man to God. The Lord wants to show us who Jesus really is: "In the beginning was the Word, and the Word was with God, and the Word was God. And the Word became flesh and dwelt among us (John 1:1, 14)." Jesus came to earth as the Word and God in human form.

We are told in Romans 3:23 that "all have sinned and fall short of the glory of God." That means we are all guilty of sin and in need of a savior. Jesus is that Savior. The penalty for sin and rebellion is death. Jesus laid down His life and took the penalty man deserves. Salvation was accomplished when He shed His blood on the cross at Calvary. The trespass of Adam brought forth sin, condemnation, and death. Belief in the sacrifice of Jesus Christ makes one righteous and frees from the bonds of sin. The fruit of Jesus Christ's life (the second Adam) brought forth grace, justification, and life.

Jesus came, died, and was resurrected from the dead through the power of the Holy Spirit. His sacrificial death on the cross gives man access to the throne of God. The blood of Jesus brings salvation, redemption, justification, reconciliation, sanctification, access to God, and daily forgiveness of our sins.

The Atoning Blood of Jesus

Central to salvation is the atoning blood of Jesus Christ. The word *atone* means to reconcile or to be reconciled to God. The blood of Christ opens the way for believers to come directly before God though Him in order to find grace, mercy, help, and salvation. "For God so loved the world, that he gave his only begotten Son, that whoever believes in him should not perish, but have everlasting life" (John 3:16). The blood of Christ offers not only forgiveness of sin but also sanctification. Sanctification, or being made holy, takes place when the mind is renewed (Romans 12:2) and conformed to the image of Christ (Romans 8:29). Sanctification is made possible because of the offering of the blood of Christ Jesus.

Sanctification by the blood of Jesus Christ brings one into a new covenant with God. Significantly, sins are eternally atoned for by the blood sacrifice of Christ on the cross. This means that the one who comes to God because of belief in Christ has an unhindered entrance to God. This is not based on the perfection of our character but upon the work of Jesus Christ, our substitute. Because the blood of Christ has been shed for us, our position in the eyes of God is secure. We are in Christ, and we are holy as He is holy (1 Corinthians 1:30) and made acceptable by God.

Salvation, Grace, and Mercy

Salvation is offered freely to all and is provided by God's grace. A person cannot be saved by works. Nor can he be saved by good deeds of love or laborious efforts to keep God's commandments. While these efforts are commendable, they cannot bring about salvation. Importantly, salvation comes from an acknowledgment that Jesus Christ came from heaven to earth to offer Himself as a sacrifice for sin. In doing so, He takes our place and releases us from the bond of sin. We also gain access to peace and eternal life with God.

> But not as the offence, so also is the free gift. For if through the offence of one many be dead, much more the grace of God, and the gift by grace, which is by one man, Jesus Christ, hath abounded unto many. (Romans 5:15)

> Even when we were dead in sins, hath quickened us together with Christ, (by grace ye are saved). (Ephesians 2:5)

> But God commendeth his love toward us, in that, while we were yet sinners, Christ died for us. (Romans 5:8)

Grace

> But he said to me, "My grace is sufficient for you, for my power is made perfect in weakness." Therefore, I will boast all the more gladly about my weaknesses, so that Christ's power may rest on me. (2 Corinthians 12:9 NIV)

The only way to salvation is by the grace of God. Grace alone. God loves, forgives, and saves us not because of who we are or what we do but because of the sacrifice of Christ on the cross. From beginning to end, salvation is by the grace of God. Faith is what causes the grace of God to be bestowed upon man (Romans 5:8). God's grace operates within believers both to will and to act according to God's good purpose (Philippians 2:12–13). To paraphrase 2 Corinthians 12:9, the Lord is the gracious and divine influencer who benefits the life of the believer. He is sufficient or all that you need.

The Holy Spirit transforms our hearts and allows grace to work in our lives. That change causes an internal altering of the heart. The outcome is that we grow toward and gain a better understanding of the knowledge, purposes, and will of God. Additionally, our wills are changed, causing us to serve the true and living God with renewed vigor. Our lifestyles and relationships have changed also.

Mercy

> But God, being rich in mercy, because of His great love
> with which He loved us, even when we were dead in
> our transgressions, made us alive together with Christ
> (by grace you have been saved). (Ephesians 2:4–5)

Mercy is the compassion of God that moved Him to provide a Savior for the unsaved. Love, on the other hand, is the motivating plan behind all that God does in saving a soul. But since God is holy and righteous, and sin is a complete offense to Him, His love or His mercy cannot operate in grace until there is provided a sufficient satisfaction for sin. This satisfaction makes possible the exercise of God's grace. Grace rules out all human merit. It requires only faith in the Savior. God's grace provides not only salvation but safety and preservation for the one saved, despite their imperfections. Grace perfects forever the saved one in the sight of God because of the saved one's position in Christ.

The Greek word that is translated as mercy in the New Testament is *eleeo* (Strong, eleeo [13]). It can also be translated as loving kindness or tender compassion. This mercy is also connected with the love of God. We are saved as a result of God's loving-kindness and tender compassion. He saved us despite the good things we did, because of his mercy. Our sins were washed away; we became heirs of God and joint heirs with Jesus Christ. We have a new life through the Holy Spirit because of the mercies of God.

The Fundamentals of Salvation

Salvation comes from an acknowledgment that Jesus Christ came from heaven to earth to offer Himself as a sacrifice for sin. In doing so, He takes our place and releases us from the bond of sin. We also gain access to peace and eternal life with God. Salvation is a gift from God. We will continue with discussions on the fundamentals of salvation.

Salvation is based upon faith in Jesus Christ and the acknowledgment that He is the Son of God.

Faith comes as the result of teaching and hearing God's Word (Romans 10:14–17). We gain knowledge and believe that Jesus paid for our sins with His blood. This causes us to have faith in Him. Faith gives us the privilege of being in covenant with God the Father. We become heirs of God and joint heirs with Christ (Romans 8:17). This secures a place of eternal privilege with the Lord. Our faith and confession of that faith grants us all the privileges of salvation.

> And she shall bring forth a son, and thou shalt call
> his name Jesus: for he shall save his people from their
> sins. (Matthew 1:21)

With salvation comes forgiveness of sin and eternal life.

Sin can be broadly defined as any attitude or action that opposes the character and will of God. Sin is what brings death—that is, separation from God. Sin also means "missing the mark" or "disobedience to God's law."

> For when ye were the servants of sin, ye were free
> from righteousness. But now being made free from
> sin, and become servants to God, ye have your
> fruit unto holiness, and the end everlasting life.
> (Romans 6:20, 22)

> If we confess our sins, he is faithful and just to
> forgive us our sins, and to cleanse us from all
> unrighteousness. (1 John 1:9)

In order to be saved, you must first admit that you are a sinner.

> For all have sinned, and come short of the glory of
> God. (Romans 3:23)

> If we confess our sins, He is faithful and just to
> forgive us our sins, and to cleanse us from all
> unrighteousness. (John 1:9)

God always takes the first steps in salvation. First, He prepares the plan for us before we were born. He then invites us to participate in His provisions of grace by calling us to salvation. You must believe in Jesus Christ as Savior of the world and your Savior, admit to God that you are a sinner, confess sins to Jesus Chris, and ask for His forgiveness.

Salvation is offered freely to all and is provided by God's grace.

The *Strong's Greek Lexicon* [14] word for grace is *charis*, which can be translated as a gift or the generosity that inspires the gift. Salvation is a gift that is expressed through love and mercy. Grace is the free favor of God, founded upon His holiness. Through grace, salvation is freely given by God to undeserving sinners.

> For by grace are ye saved through faith; and that not of yourselves: it is the gift of God: Not of works, lest any man should boast. For we are his workmanship, created in Christ Jesus unto good works, which God hath before ordained that we should walk in them. (Ephesians 2:8–10).

> But not as the offence, so also is the free gift. For if through the offence of one many be dead, much more the grace of God, and the gift by grace, which is by one man, Jesus Christ, hath abounded unto many. (Romans 5:15)

Those who acknowledge that Jesus is the Son of God also believe that He paid the penalty for our sins through His death on the cross.

Jesus died the painful death for our sins by sacrificing Himself for us on the cross. In order to be forgiven for sin, one must acknowledge that Jesus died for our sins. Acknowledging sins offers the blessing of being born again and receiving eternal life with Christ.

For it became him, for whom are all things, and by whom are all things, in bringing many sons unto glory, to make the captain of their salvation perfect through sufferings. (Hebrews 2:10)

God did not send the Son into the world to condemn the world, but in order that the world might be saved through him. (John 3:17)

For God made Christ, who never sinned, to be the offering for our sin, so that we could be made right with God through Christ. (2 Corinthians 5:21 NLT)

Salvation is accompanied by repentance, redemption, regeneration, justification, and peace with god.

Repentance

Through the atonement of Jesus Christ, our Father in heaven has provided the only way for us to be forgiven of our sins. Christ suffered the penalty for our sins so we can be forgiven if we sincerely repent. As we repent and rely on His redeeming quality, we will be cleansed from sin. Sin makes one unclean and unworthy to be in the presence of God. Repentance shows a total turn away from sin. When one repents, he turns from sin and turns to God. This is accomplished by asking God for forgiveness for sin.

Repent, then, and turn to God, so that your sins may be wiped out, that times of refreshing may come from the Lord. (Acts 3:19)

If we confess our sins, he is faithful and just and will forgive us our sins and purify us from all unrighteousness. (1 John 1:9)

The Lord is not slow in keeping his promise, as some understand slowness. Instead he is patient with you, not wanting anyone to perish, but everyone to come to repentance. (2 Peter 3:9)

Redemption

Redemption means to be free from the slavery of Satan and sin's dominion. To redeem someone is to recover him from the hands of aliens. In the Christian sense, redemption is secured by the price of Christ's precious blood. It is through this ransom that the Christian experiences deliverance from the world, Satan, sin, self, and death and receives righteousness and everlasting life.

In him we have redemption through his blood, the forgiveness of our trespasses, according to the riches of his grace; wherein He hath abounded toward us in all wisdom and prudence. (Ephesians 1:7–8)

Blessed be the God and Father of our Lord Jesus Christ, who hath blessed us with all spiritual blessings in heavenly places in Christ: According as he hath chosen us in him before the foundation of the world, that we should be holy and without blame before him in love: Having predestinated us unto the adoption of children by Jesus Christ to himself, according to the good pleasure of his will, To the praise of the glory of his grace, wherein he hath made us accepted in the beloved. In whom we have redemption through his blood, the forgiveness of sins, according to the riches of his grace. (Ephesians 1:3–7)

Apostle Paul stated in verse 3 of chapter 1 of Ephesians that we are blessed by God, the Father of our Lord Jesus, with "all spiritual blessings in heavenly places in Christ." Redemption is one of those spiritual blessings. Redemption means that a price was paid to deliver mankind from the bondage of Satan. The price was the blood of Jesus Christ.

Christ hath redeemed us from the curse of the law, being made a curse for us: for it is written, Cursed is everyone that hangeth on a tree. (Galatians 3:13)

Regeneration

Regeneration is the work of the Holy Spirit bringing one into union with Christ. We were dead spiritually but made alive through faith in Christ Jesus. A new life is implanted into the life of a born-again Christian. The Holy Spirit is given to the believer as a down payment of what we are going to have in greater fullness in the future. His presence and work in our lives lead us to victory, both as a sanctifier and a comforter. We receive the spirit of wisdom and revelation to help us draw near to God through the presence of the Holy Spirit. The Holy Spirit builds the body of Christ and motivates unity in the faith. Significantly, the Holy Spirit fills and empowers believers and helps in prayer and spiritual warfare.

Therefore, if any man be in Christ, he is a new creature: old things are passed away; behold, all things are become new. (2 Corinthians 5:17)

Justification

Justification means deliverance from condemnation and declared not guilty in God's sight. It is based on faith in the redemptive power of belief in Christ Jesus and the redemptive power of the cross. Significantly, God sees believers as He sees His own Son, by our identification with Him by the baptism of the Holy Spirit. We are members of His body, and He accepts us as He accepts Jesus Christ. This justification is the believer's eternal standing.

> Being justified freely by his grace through the redemption that is in Christ Jesus. (Romans 3:24)

Peace with God

Salvation comes from an acknowledgment that Jesus Christ came down from heaven to earth to offer Himself as a sacrifice for sin. In doing so, He takes our place and releases us from the bond of sin. We also gain access to peace and eternal life with God. Peace comes to us when we accept the Lord Jesus as our Savior. Peace with God is a product of God's grace. He loves us and wants us to experience the peace that comes by means of salvation. The ultimate source of peace is eternal life with God.

> Therefore, being justified by faith, we have peace with God through our Lord Jesus Christ: By whom also we have access by faith into this grace wherein we stand, and rejoice in hope of the glory of God. (Romans 5:1–2)

> But of him are ye in Christ Jesus, who of God is made unto us wisdom, and righteousness, and sanctification, and redemption. (1 Corinthians 1:30)

Righteousness

The word *righteous* is used in two different ways in the Bible. Righteousness as a way of living in holiness. This definition is found in Ephesians 2:13 and will be referred to as *righteousness acts.*

Righteousness is also mentioned in the Bible as having right standing with God because of faith in the offering of His Son, Jesus Christ, to die for the sins of man. The scriptural reference is found in Hebrews 8:2: It is made possible because the sins of man were exchanged for the perfect righteousness of Christ. This is referred to as *righteousness gained as a result of believing in and accepting Christ as Savior.*

> But now you have been united with Christ Jesus. Once you were far away from God, but now you have been brought near to him through the blood of Christ. (Ephesians 2:13 NLT)

> For I will be merciful to their unrighteousness, and their sins and their iniquities will I remember no more. (Hebrews 8:2)

Righteousness is referred to as righteous acts.

God is all light; He is perfect in purity and holiness. God is infinitely holy. Holiness is an attribute of God. He is righteous, blameless, and perfect. Isaiah the prophet saw the Lord in His holiness and perfection in Isaiah 6:3 and proclaimed, "Holy, holy, holy, is the Lord of hosts: the whole earth is full of His glory." When speaking of the Lord's righteousness, a writer in Psalm 119:139 declares, "Righteous are you, O Lord, and right are your rules." The first chapter of Psalms proclaims the righteous person as someone who does not live in the counsel of the wicked, nor sits in the seat of the ungodly, but delights and joys in God's law.

Righteousness Gained by Accepting Christ as Savior

Man was created to glorify God and to enjoy fellowship with Him. God's purpose in saving us is to bring us back into right relationship with Him. This type of relationship symbolizes fellowship. When Jesus died on the cross, He bore all sins of humanity and became sin for us. As a result, everyone who believes in Jesus Christ is made righteous with God. The relationship between God and man, which was broken because of the sin of Adam, was restored through the sacrifice of Jesus. He was the Lamb of God who took away the sins of the world. Believing in Him is the work of faith. Faith produces righteousness.

> For what saith the scripture? Abraham believed God, and it was counted unto him for righteousness. Now to him that worketh is the reward not reckoned of grace, but of debt. But to him that worketh not, but believeth on him that justifieth the ungodly, his faith is counted for righteousness. Even as David also describeth the blessedness of the man, unto whom God imputeth righteousness without works. This righteousness is given through faith in Jesus Christ to all who believe. There is no difference between Jew and Gentile. (Romans 4:3–6)

If You Are Not Saved, This Is Your Call to Salvation

God always takes the first steps in salvation. He prepares the plan, and then He invites men to participate in His provisions of grace. If you are not saved, this is your call to salvation.

1. Admit to God that you are a sinner.
    For all have sinned and come short of the glory of God. (Romans 3:23)

2. Believe in Jesus Christ as Savior of the world and your Savior.
    For God so loved the world, that He gave His only begotten Son, that whosoever believeth in Him should not perish, but have everlasting life. (John 3:16)

3. Confess your sins to Jesus Christ and ask for His forgiveness.
    If we confess our sins, He is faithful and just to forgive us our sins, and to cleanse us from all unrighteousness. (1 John 1:9)

Repeat This Prayer for Salvation

Heavenly Father, I know that I am a sinner, and I need Your forgiveness. Jesus died on the cross for my sins, and I receive Him as my Savior and Lord. I thank You that He arose again for my justification. I ask You to forgive my sins and bring me into fellowship with You. Please take my life and make me what You want me to be. I thank you in Jesus's name. Amen.

If you prayed this prayer, you can be certain that the Lord heard you. You can also be certain of your salvation. The first thing that you need to do now is ask God to help you find a place to worship Him and grow with other Christian in a church that will assist you in developing in God through His Word, the Bible. Then tell others and invite them to fellowship into the kingdom of our God. I guarantee you will find rest and peace in your soul. Continue reading this book so that you will learn to develop an intimate and productive spiritual life. Hallelujah! God Bless you, and I love you.

THE LORD HAS PROVIDED US AN EXTRAORDINARY LIFE THAT IS FAR BEYOND ANYTHING WE CAN ASK FOR OR EVEN THINK ABOUT.

Word Seed: "if we ask anything according to His will, He hears us. And if we know that he hear us, whatsoever we ask, we know that we have the petitions that we desired of him" (1 John 5:14–15).

The Seed of the Word

As part of the Lord's Prayer, Jesus taught us to pray, "Thy will be done in earth, as it is in heaven" (Matthew 6:10b). God's will is His Word. His Word contains His promises of living an abundant life. God cannot lie; His promises stand firm (Titus 1:2, Isaiah 41:10). However, many of His promises come with conditions. Our key scripture is one of them. Let us review a similar scripture, John 15:7. It reads, "If ye abide in me, and my words abide in you, ye shall ask what ye will, and it shall be done unto you." To abide in Christ is to is to live in Him, get to know Him, depend on Him, be obedient to His Word, and allow His Word to transform our lives.

The Action of the Word

Word Seed: "Blessed are those who obey his laws and search for him with all their hearts. They do not compromise with evil, and they walk only in his paths" (Psalm 119:2–3).

Things can be in disarray all around us, but we still live an extraordinary life in the Lord. That is because peace and joy in the Lord come from within. It is not about everything else that is happening around us. Psalm 119:2–3 describes four ways by which we can be blessed and live abundant and extraordinary lives: 1) obey God's Word; 2) take time to search for and know Him; 3) don't compromise good for evil; and 4) walk according to God's will. "Blessed are those who obey his laws and search for him with all their hearts. They do not compromise with evil, and they walk only in his paths."

The Persistence of the Word

The abundant life began at salvation. It is more than wealth, prosperity, and riches. It is an overall blessed life that is empowered by the Holy Spirit and provides exceedingly abundant blessing, far better than we could ever imagine (Ephesians 3:20). The thief is the destroyer in our lives who comes to steal our joy and peace by trying to prevent us from receiving the full blessings of salvation. Jesus Christ came to free us from the bondages of sin and to provide us with a life of peace, joy, fulfillment, and abundance here on earth.

What Is This Word Saying to You?

SALVATION: YOU MUST BE BORN AGAIN

Word Seed: "For by grace are ye saved through faith; and that not of yourselves: it is the gift of God: not of works, lest any man should boast" (Ephesians 2:8–9).

The Seed of the Word

The word *salvation* comes from the Greek word *soteria*,[15] which means "deliverance, preservation and safety." It primarily involves deliverance from the bondage of sin (Galatians 5:1) but also includes deliverance from enemies (Luke 1:71) and from sickness and disease (Isaiah 53:4; 1 Peter 2:24). Salvation is a gift made available to those who repent, believe, and confess their belief that Jesus is Lord and that He died and rose from the dead to save mankind (Acts 16:31, Romans10:9–10). The gift cannot be earned through good deeds or by simply being a "good person" (Ephesians 2:8–9). It is a matter of being spiritually renewed and becoming a child of God through faith. "Therefore, if anyone is in Christ, he is a new creation, the old has gone, and the new has come" (1 Corinthians 5:17).

The Action of the Word

Word Seed: "God has sent His only begotten Son into the world, that we might live through Him. In this is love, not that we loved God, but that He loved us and sent His Son to be the propitiation for our sins" (1 John 4:9–10).

God's love for man was so great that "He gave His only begotten Son, that whosoever believeth in Him should not perish, but have everlasting life" (John 3:16). Jesus came to save us from sin, so that we "can have life and have it more abundantly" (John 10:10b). By paying the blood price for man's sin, He made direct access to God possible. Salvation is offered to all and provided by God's grace (Ephesians 2:8–9). It is accompanied by redemption, regeneration, justification, and peace with God. Redemption frees one from sin and gives righteousness and everlasting life. "Blessed be the God and Father of our Lord Jesus Christ, who has blessed us with every spiritual blessing in the heavenly places in Christ" (Ephesians 1:3).

The Persistence of the Word

Being saved does not only involve what Christ did for us; it also involves what He does in us. The Lord works in each of us every day to transform us into the image of Christ and to make us more like Him. We are told how this is achieved in Ezekiel 36:26–27: "I will give you a new heart and put a new spirit within you, I will remove the heart of stone from your flesh and give you a heart of flesh. And I will put my Spirit within you and cause you to walk in my statutes."

What Is This Word Saying to You?

THE CROSS, REPENTANCE, SALVATION, AND ENCOUNTERING THE DAMASCUS ROAD

Word Seed: "Who Himself (Christ) bore our sins in His own body on the cross, that we, having died to sins, might live for righteousness—by whose stripes you were healed" (1 Peter 2:24).

The Seed of the Word

Romans 5:8 says, "But God demonstrates His own love toward us, in that while we were yet sinners, Christ died for us." Jesus gave His life, a life of perfection, without sin, so that we can be saved. It is by His shed blood that salvation is now made possible for all humans. We cannot earn salvation. We are saved by God's grace when we have faith in His Son, Jesus Christ. If you are not saved, would you receive God's gift of love today? You must believe you are a sinner and that Christ died for your sins and is Lord (Romans 10:9). Ask His forgiveness. Then turn from your sins; this is called repentance. Finally, ask the Lord to come into your heart and live His life in you and through you (Romans 8:10, Galatians 2:20).

The Action of the Word

"For God so loved the world that He gave His one and only Son, that whoever believes in Him shall not perish but have eternal life" (John 3:16). The message of the cross is that Christ died and rose again so that all who believe on His name would not perish but have everlasting life. And those who believe in Him are placed in union with Him by the power of the Holy Spirit. We are the body of Christ, and we are identified with Him—and He with us.

The Persistence of the Word

"That the God of our Lord Jesus Christ, the Father of glory, may give unto you the spirit of wisdom and revelation in the knowledge of him" (Ephesians1:17). This is the prayer that apostle Paul prayed for all of God's children. He prayed that we may grow in grace and wisdom, be increased in understanding and knowledge of God, and receive greater illumination and spiritual revelation of His Son, Jesus Christ, who died for our sins and rose again the third day to give us His abundant life, according to the riches of His grace.

What Is This Word Saying to You?

OH, TASTE AND SEE THAT
THE LORD IS GOOD!

Word Seed: "O taste and see that the Lord is good: blessed is the man that trusteth in him" (Psalm 34:8).

The Seed of the Word

No matter what is happening in the world around us, God is good. His presence is always with us. David knew that as he was being pursued by King Saul and his men. He had experienced the goodness of God throughout his life. That is why he could say, "Surely goodness and mercy shall follow me all the days of my life" (Psalm 23:6). Tasting involves testing and experiencing for ourselves the fact that God is good. We are invited to come near Him so that we can experience His nearness, deliverance, salvation, and redemption for ourselves. When we do, we will find that there is no difficulty, defeat, or circumstance in our lives that cannot be redeem for God's good purpose. His goodness is there for us, and His mercy will never leave us.

The Action of the Word

We read in Genesis 1:31 that after creating the heavens and the earth, "God created man and woman in His image and likeness and gave them dominion over all that He had created" (Genesis 1:28). However, Adam and Eve stopped trusting God's goodness and made their own decisions about what was right and wrong. This disobedience led to sin, spiritual death, and separation from God. But God is good and faithful in His character. And despite man's disobedience and failures, God does not fail, forget, weaken, change, or disappoint. Importantly, He cannot be persuaded to alter

His Word or talked into answering selfish prayer (Psalm 89:34). Without His goodness, we would all remain in the fallen state caused by the Fall in the Garden of Eden. However, because of His grace, His mercy, and His loving-kindness, what was lost at the Fall was reclaimed at the cross.

The Persistence of the Word

Although our circumstances change, God never changes. James 1:17 assures us that God "does not change like shifting shadows," and God himself declares in Malachi 3:6, "I do not change." God sent His Son, Jesus Christ, to die on the cross and take the penalty of our sin, reconciling us to Himself and making eternal life with Him possible.

What Is This Word Saying to You?

FAITH, MEEKNESS, AND TEMPERANCE

Word Seed: "That Christ may dwell in your hearts by faith" (Ephesians 2:17a; also read Ephesians 3:16–19).

The Seed of the Word

Christ begins to live in our hearts when we put our trust in Him through salvation. As we study the Bible, our knowledge of God grows, and our faith gets stronger. The more we put our faith to work, the more developed our character becomes. This leads us to change from our old ways so we can become more like Jesus. Faithfulness of character is expressed the same, whether in public, private, at home, or at church. This means that our whole inner life—thoughts, feelings, motives, and intentions—are influenced and strengthened by the Word of God. That's why apostle Paul prayed that the Lord would "strengthen us with might by his Spirit in the inner man; and that we would be rooted and grounded in love, so that we may be able to comprehend with all saints what is the breadth, and length, and depth, and height; and to know the love of Christ, which passes knowledge, that we might be filled with all the fulness of God" (Ephesians 3:16–19).

The Action of the Word

"Blessed Are the Meek, for They Will Inherit the Earth" (Matthew 5:5). Both gentleness and meekness are classified as fruit of the Spirt. Gentleness refers mostly to actions: quietness, kindness, calmness, and compassion. On the other hand, meekness refers to attitude: patience, being in control when faced with adversity, being grateful, and having a teachable and humble spirit. Meekness is often described as "having power under control." Being gentle and meek is not popular in today's culture. God calls us out of darkness to set the right examples and to be "the light of the world" (Matthew 5:14).

The Persistence of the Word

"And everyone who competes for the prize is temperate in all things. Now they do it to obtain a perishable crown, but we for an imperishable crown" (1 Corinthians 9:25). Temperance requires self-discipline. It means being able to master your own desires and passions. This means that we are to be Christ controlled and under the authority of the Holy Spirit. Every believer who exercises self-control for the sake of Christ is promised an imperishable, incorruptible crown that will never ever fade away (1 Corinthians 9:25).

What Is This Word Saying to You?

THE FRUIT OF LOVE

Word Seed: "Love is patient, love is kind. It does not envy, it does not boast, it is not proud. It is not rude, it is not self-seeking, it is not easily angered, it keeps no record of wrongs" (1 Corinthians 13:4–5).

The Seed of the Word

Romans 12:21 says, "Be not overcome of evil, but overcome evil with good." It takes the fruit of love to fulfill this requirement. The fruit of love is not triggered by emotion but by allowing the Holy Spirit to impart His love in us. Verse 6 of this chapter says, "Love does not delight in evil but rejoices with the truth." Apostle Paul did not include the word *nice* in this passage. However, he did say that love is "kind." Niceness is outwardly focused on avoiding conflict and keeping friends. Kindness comes from the inside and is a desire for the salvation, well-being, and building up of others. Love should always seek to build up others, but that does not mean ignoring sin or not calling out evil or wrong intent in others.

The Action of the Word

The love of God reaches into every part of believers' lives and touches every jot and tittle of our need. It is the very foundation of our walk with Christ. "Whoever does not love does not know God, because GOD IS LOVE" (1 John 4:8). The person who continues in love is also continuing in God. As we become aware of and familiar with God's love for us, our love grows, matures, and begins to look more like His love for us. We then begin to seek to meet the needs of others without compensation. Jesus explained this kind of love when He said, "Love your enemies, and do good, and lend, expecting nothing in return; and your reward will be great, and you will be sons of the Most High; for He Himself is kind to ungrateful and evil men" (Luke 6:35).

The Persistence of the Word

It is only through God working in us that we can genuinely love one another. And it is only through the Holy Spirit that hearts are changed and drawn to the Father. Jesus set an example for us to love (John 13:34–35; 1 John 3:16–20). He took the role of a servant and placed the needs of others above His own dignity when He washed His disciples' feet. He then instructed them to do the same (John 13:1–17). This kind of love is not a feeling but a choice. It is the choice to be kind, to sacrifice, to consider others' needs greater than one's own (Philippians 2:3).

What Is This Word Saying to You?

FAITH WORKS BY LOVE

Word Seed: "For in Christ Jesus neither circumcision nor uncircumcision avails anything, but faith working through love" (Galatians 5:6).

The Seed of the Word

Many Christians work and struggle all their lives, hoping to please God. However, we cannot accomplish things in the spirit on our own efforts. Hebrews 11:6 reads, "But without faith it is impossible to please him: for he that cometh to God must believe that he is, and that he is a rewarder of them that diligently seek him." Faith is connected to the love that we have for God and for one another. Love transforms us. The result of that transformation is the fulfillment of God's Word (faith). Faith takes guilt, fear, greed, and covetousness from the heart and gives us an appetite for loving God and experiencing the joy of His Word moving in our lives.

The Action of the Word

Spiritual gifts are meaningless when practiced without love (1 Corinthians 13:1–2). Love is the foundation of life, because "God is love" (1 John 4:8). Faith works when we realize how much God loves us. His love is not based on our performance. God's love is independent of the circumstances that we face in life. The more we understand His love for us, the more we will see faith working in our lives. "What then shall we say to these things? If God is for us, who can be against us? He who did not spare His own Son, but delivered Him up for us all, how shall He not with Him also freely give us all things" (Romans 8:31–32).

The Persistence of the Word

Jesus explains how we should love in two passages of scripture: We are to love God and our neighbors (Matthew 22:37–39). We are also to love others as God loves us (John 13:34–35). Compared to faith and hope, spiritual gifts and sacrifices have little value if they are not motivated by love for God and for others. Faith and hope are important. Faith pleases God (Hebrews 11:6). Most important, it takes faith to believe that God loves us and that He provides for our needs. Hope helps to anchor our souls in times of need and is the confident expectation of God's faithfulness to His promises. Faith and hope will not be needed in the eternal, but love is everlasting. God is love.

What Is This Word Saying to You?

REDEMPTION

Word Seed: "Forasmuch as ye know that ye were not redeemed with corruptible things, as silver and gold, from your vain conversation received by tradition from your fathers; But with the precious blood of Christ, as of a lamb without blemish and without spot" (1 Peter 1:18–19).

The Seed of the Word

Sermons on the explicit topics of redemption or blood are not taught much these days. However, redemption is the foundation of our salvation and the basis on which most sermons are built. Redemption refers to the deliverance of man from sin. To be redeemed is to be forgiven, justified, and reconciled to God. Romans 5:8–10 explains it this way: "But God demonstrates his own love for us in this: While we were still sinners, Christ died for us. Since we have now been justified by his blood, how much more shall we be saved from God's wrath through him! For if, while we were God's enemies, we were reconciled to him through the death of his Son, how much more, having been reconciled, shall we be saved through his life!"

The Action of the Word

"The Father has "delivered us from the power of darkness, and hath translated us into the kingdom of his dear Son: In whom we have redemption through his blood, even the forgiveness of sins" (Colossians 1:13–14). Salvation is not only about having our sins forgiven but also about becoming able to see God's glory. "For God, who said let light shine out of darkness, made his light shine in our hearts to give us the light of the knowledge of the glory of God in the face of Christ" (2 Corinthians 4:6). God's love for man was so great that He sent His only begotten Son to be our substitute for sin. Jesus Christ is our "light of life," in whom we have received forgiveness of sins, in accordance with the riches of God's grace (Ephesians 1:7).

The Persistence of the Word

Love is the true characteristic of God. He is love. Love is the heart of His nature. We are saved because of His love. Apart from God's love there would be no redemption or salvation (Ephesians 2:4–7). The greatest expression of God's love for us is found in John 3:16: "For God so loved the world that he gave His only begotten Son, that whoever believes in him shall not perish but have eternal life."

What Is This Word Saying to You?

HOPE IN GOD

Word Seed: "Why, I ask myself, are you so depressed? Why are you so upset inside? Hope in God!" (Psalm 42:5 CEB).

The Seed of the Word

Most of us know what it is like to sit in darkness and wonder if light will ever come. However, we all know that light will eventually come. We do not have to wait until it is light. The secret place is where God dwells (Psalm 18:11). We read in the first chapter that everything began from God's secret place: "And the earth was without form, and void; and darkness was upon the face of the deep. And the Spirit of God moved upon the face of the waters." Our secret place can be in our prayer closet. Luke 6:12–13 tells us that Jesus also made darkness His prayer closet: "Now it came to pass in those days that He went out to the mountain to pray and continued all night in prayer to God. And when it was day, He called His disciples to Himself."

The Action of the Word

"I pray that the eyes of your heart may be enlightened, so that you will know what is the hope of His calling, what are the riches of the glory of His inheritance in the saints, and what is the boundless greatness of His power toward us who believe" (Ephesians 1:18–19b NASB). The more understanding that we have of God's love through Christ, and the more we meditate and praise God for it, the greater our hope becomes. To summarize it, God's love is something we can never exhaust, and its depths are immeasurable. This is the love that Paul prays for God's people.

The Persistence of the Word

God has blessed each Christian with "every spiritual blessing in the heavenly places in Christ." That does not mean that we automatically experience these blessings. The main reason is that we do not always have a full understanding of what these blessings are when we are initially saved. Even though God has opened our eyes to see and believe in Jesus Christ as Savior and Lord, we still must seek Him to enlighten the eyes of our hearts so that we will come to a deeper understanding of all of His truths. Our spiritual understanding must grow every day; otherwise, we will go into reversion in our spiritual life.

What Is This Word Saying to You?

THE LIFE-GIVING POWER OF GOD'S WORD

Word Seed: "The LORD said to me, 'You have seen correctly, for I am watching to see that my word is fulfilled" (Jeremiah 1:12 NIV).

The Seed of the Word

Nothing is impossible with respect to any of God's promises. Significantly, "no word from Him shall be without power or fulfillment" (Luke 1:37b AMP, classic edition). There is often a gap between seeing a promise of God in His Word and experiencing the fulfillment of that promise. That is because some of the promises in the Bible are conditional. We must meet the conditions of those promises before they are fulfilled in our lives. We must also be aware that God's promises are based on His perfect timing and purposes. For example, the desire to get married is a good one. However, God's slowness in fulfilling that promise may be His way of giving us something better or keeping up from making a terrible mistake.

The Action of the Word

Hebrews 4:12–13 reads, "For the word of God is alive and active. Sharper than any double-edged sword, it penetrates even to dividing soul and spirit, joints, and marrow; it judges the thoughts and attitudes of the heart. Nothing in all creation is hidden from God's sight. Everything is uncovered and laid bare before the eyes of him to whom we must give account." God's Word has power to convert sinners and build up God's people by exposing our sin and pointing to God's grace at the cross. The Word has life-producing effects and helps us to see our true selves.

The Persistence of the Word

God's Word will never fail. His promises are firm and unfailing. Our unbelief and lack of knowledge can prevent its fulfilment in our lives. All things in life go through seasons; things come, and things go. We can see that in nature. The grass begins to wither during the fall. Additionally, flowers lose their beauty, and tree leaves start wasting and fall to the ground. The other seasons, winter, spring, and summer, have natural occurrences that happen annually. But God does not change. He sits calmly and unmoved, regardless of the changes that occur on earth. His promises are faithful, His warnings are not empty threats, and He offers salvation to all who come to Him in faith (Lamentations 2:17a NIV).

What Is This Word Saying to You?

RIGHTEOUSNESS AND PEACE

Word Seed: "And when Jesus was baptized, immediately he went up from the water, and behold, the heavens were opened to him, and he saw the Spirit of God descending like a dove and coming to rest on him; and behold, a voice from heaven said, 'This is my beloved Son, with whom I am well pleased'" (Matthew 3:16–17).

The Seed of the Word

The manifestation of the Father, Son, and Holy Spirit was revealed at Jesus's baptism. The key scripture states that the heavenly Father spoke over His Son with affirmation from heaven, and the Holy Spirit descended upon Him from heaven as a dove. The dove is a symbol of peace and has symbolized peace between God and human beings, going back to the time of the flood (Genesis 8:8–12). The angels proclaimed that God's peace had come to the earth at Jesus's birth (Luke 2:14). Everything that He did was done under the power and anointing of the Holy Spirit. If Jesus needed the Holy Spirit, how much more so do we? When we believe in Him, we are justified, through faith, and have peace with God (Romans 5:1).

The Action of the Word

Isaiah 32:17 reads, "And the work of righteousness shall be peace; and the effect of righteousness quietness and assurance forever." Jesus is the king of righteousness. His work of righteousness was manifested when he died on the cross of Calvary. Significantly, He, the Prince of Peace, left His Holy Spirit to lead and guide us into all truth. His Word is truth (John 17:1). And it is by the Word of truth that God sanctifies us.

The Persistence of the Word

Jesus said, "Peace I leave with you; my peace I give you. I do not give to you as the world gives. Do not let your hearts be troubled and do not be afraid" (John 14:27). If we review this scripture closely, we will find both a promise from Christ and a life-giving command. He promises that He will leave His peace for us as a gift, and He commands us to not be troubled and afraid in this world. His promise is supported by the presence of the Holy Spirit, who will "will teach you all things and will remind you of everything I have said to you" (John 14:26). We must fill our hearts with courage and peace by going to the Father and reading His Word daily.

What Is This Word Saying to You?

GROW IN GRACE AND IN KNOWLEDGE

Word Seed: "But grow in the grace and knowledge of the Lord Jesus Christ" (2 Peter 3:18).

The Seed of the Word

"We are saved by grace through faith" (Ephesians 2:8–9). Sanctification means to set aside or to be made holy. We grow in grace by reading God's Word and letting it "dwell in us richly" (Colossians 3:16). Growth is a lifelong process of becoming like Jesus. However, the amount of growth depends on our study and application of God's Word (2 Timothy 3:16–17). Significantly, we are responsible to make the choice to become transformed into Christ's image. We do this by letting go of the things that keep us in bondage to sin.

The Action of the Word

Grace is the "unmerited favor" we received through Jesus's sacrifice on the cross for our sin. Growing in grace means coming to a greater understanding of God's holiness, justice, and sovereignty. To grow in grace does not mean we receive more grace from God. We received all the grace we needed at salvation (2 Peter 1:3). How do we grow in grace and knowledge? Knowledge can be defined as information that leads to understanding and results in application. True knowledge comes from God. We grow in knowledge when we apply what we learn from God's Word. By growing in our knowledge of Christ and in His abundant grace, we are enabled to live the "abundant life" he came to give us (John 10:10; 2 Corinthians 9:8).

The Persistence of the Word

Growth is important to salvation. A person will either grow in grace or degenerate spiritually (2 Peter 3:17–18). Accepting Christ as "Lord" means that you honor Him as ruler and master of your entire life. Tony Evans says it this way: "Jesus as Lord means that Jesus is to be the one and only supreme ruler and master in your life. He calls the shots, and He is to be acknowledged in everything that is done." Believing Christ as Savior does not always lead to honoring Him as Lord of your life. To make Jesus Lord is to repent of self-centeredness and live a kingdom-centered life that depends on conforming to Christ's image.

What Is This Word Saying to You?

LIVING THE FAITH WALK

Word Seed: "For we walk by faith, not by sight" (2 Corinthians 5:7).

The Seed of the Word

Believers are called to be different. Living a godly life in an ungodly world is realizing that we do not belong to ourselves but to Jesus. He is the Shepherd of our souls. We must let our lights shine bright instead of growing dim with the world around us, so that people can see Jesus through us as we share the message of God's Word. Matthew 5:16 admonishes us to "Let your light so shine before men, that they may see your good works, and glorify your Father which is in heaven" (Matthew 5:16). How we live our lives is dominated by what we know and believe. This means that we do not disregard the things we can see; it means we let the Word of God dictate the decisions we make.

The Action of the Word

We are all aware that we live in a broken and fallen world where sin, death, and the enemy are waging war against God and anyone who stands up for truth. Faith is the ability to believe outside of what we see and hear and to look at situations through the nature and character of God (Romans 10:17). God gives every person a measure or degree of faith. He does this because He knows it is impossible to please Him without walking by faith (Romans 12:3).

The Persistence of the Word

God's will in His Word is given to show us the difference between good and evil. Without it, we would not know right from wrong

(Romans 4:15). That is why we can find peace of mind knowing our faith is from God and that He will finish the good work He started in us (Philippians 1:6). "Behold, I am coming soon! My reward is with me, and I will give to everyone according to what he has done" (Revelation 22:12). Walking by faith means we are to use our faith to live for God and to serve and encourage each other (1 Peter 4:10–11). We are to also minister and witness to unbelievers (Matthew 28:19–20). There is great reward is doing that.

What Is This Word Saying to You?

CONFIDENCE IN THE PRESENCE OF GOD

Word Seed: "According to the eternal purpose which he purposed in Christ Jesus our Lord: In whom we have boldness and access with confidence by the faith of him. Because of Christ and our faith in him, we can now come boldly and confidently into God's presence" (Ephesians 3: 11–12).

The Seed of the Word

Confidence means depending completely upon God and resting on His promises. On the other hand, lack of confidence comes from focusing on what others think of you or allowing negative feedback or situations to undermine your confidence in yourself. Therefore, confidence should never be rooted in who we are, the opinions of others, or material possessions or money. Importantly, confidence comes from being assured that God loves you, accepts you, and approves of you. "I have strength for all things in Christ Who empowers me [I am ready for anything and equal to anything through Him Who infuses inner strength into me; I am self-sufficient in Christ's sufficiency]" (Philippians 4:13 AMP).

The Action of the Word

True confidence is always rooted in God and the sacrificial death of Jesus Christ on the cross (Hebrews 10:19–22). It comes from abiding in Him and believing that you can do whatever His Word says you can do (1 John 2:2–8). The important thing is to always keep in mind that confidence in our salvation is based and rooted in obedience. The hard work has already been done through the sacrifice of our Lord and Savior Jesus Christ, who has made a one-time sacrifice for sins and serves in heaven as high priest to make reconciliation between God and man (Hebrews 10:1–10).

The Persistence of the Word

The Lord does not want us to go through this life guessing and doubting our salvation. He wants us to rest in Him and have confidence in Him, not in ourselves. He will "work all things for our good" (Romans 8:28) and has a perfect plan for our lives. And He will move heaven and earth to accomplish His plan for us. We can rest in Him, knowing that He sees more than we can see, has a higher perspective concerning our lives and futures (Isaiah55:8–9), and knows what is best for us.

What Is This Word Saying to You?

5

SPIRITUAL GROWTH
AND MATURITY

THE INDWELLING PRESENCE OF THE HOLY SPIRIT IS GIVEN TO everyone upon conversion. He is there to lead us, guide us, and help us to obey God's Word. The Holy Spirit also channels our hearts and minds toward the things of God and allows us to hear, receive from, and converse with God. When He leads, the Holy Spirit lures into prayer and worship. It is then that we are inspired by the scripture to receive the truth, the ways, and will of God for our lives. Certainly, we are all familiar with the repeating incidences that call for us to use the spiritual weapons of the Holy Spirit to combat the spiritual forces of evil that are commonplace in our lives. Meaningfully, we fellowship with God daily because we are grateful for His protection, provisions, blessings, and especially His Son, Jesus Christ.

Focusing on God should be a natural habit of the child of God. We should all be conversing with the Lord throughout the day in one form or another. It could be a situation where we are thanking Him for a particular event or circumstance that has or will be occurring in our lives. We are constantly interceding or petitioning the Lord on our own behalf or on behalf of others for things we need in life.

> "And I will pray the Father, and he shall give you another Comforter, that he may abide with you forever; Even the Spirit of truth; whom the world cannot receive, because it seeth him not, neither knoweth him: but ye know him; for he dwelleth with you, and shall be in you. I will not leave you comfortless: I will come to you." (John 14:16–18)

Hiding the Word in the Heart (Soil)

The Lord says in the tenth chapter of Hebrews and the sixteenth verse that He will make a covenant with His people and put His laws into their hearts and their minds, because He knew that it was impossible for man to keep His laws on their own. This is the New Testament Covenant promise of blood that is based upon faith. This covenant promise was fulfilled with Jesus's sacrifice for our sins on the cross of Calvary.

Hiding God's Word in the heart causes the Holy Spirit to bring it to mind during times when needed. The Word becomes a "balm." Balm is the medicine that is produced by the Holy Spirit to bring peace, comfort, and assistance to the believer. The hidden Word Seeds may also produce thoughts that will remind us that "all things work together for the good" for those who trust God, when we need that reminder. Similarly, a "quiet voice" may tell us that we do not have to be anxious about anything and remind us that "the peace of God, which transcends all understanding, will guard our hearts and your minds in Christ Jesus" (Romans 8:28; Philippians 4:6–7).

The Bible is the Word of God (Jesus). It produces seeds that harvest crops of righteousness. The measure and quality of the harvest is dependent on the condition of the heart.

This truth is found in Matthew 12:23, where Jesus explained, "Seed falling on good soil refers to someone who hears the word and understands it. This is the one who produces a crop, yielding a hundred, sixty or thirty times what was sown."

The function of the seed is to reproduce its own kind. Likewise, the Lord reproduces His own kind by planting seeds in our hearts. To be spiritually matured is to keep the Word of God as a priority of the heart. Obedience becomes an obligation; holiness becomes a commitment. Matured Christians are motivated to obey God's Word and are always willing to confess sins and live a life of holiness.

> The law of the LORD is perfect, refreshing the soul. The statutes of the LORD are trustworthy, making wise the simple. The precepts of the LORD are right, giving joy to the heart. The commands of the LORD are radiant, giving light to the eyes. The fear of the LORD is pure, enduring forever. The decrees of the LORD are firm, and all of them are righteous. (Psalm 19:7–9)

> Thy word have I hid in mine heart, that I might not sin against thee. (Psalm119: 11)

Spiritual Maturity

To be holy is to be set apart for God's service. God is holy. Holiness is one of His attributes, and because He is holy, we are to be holy also. Being obedient is a characteristic of holiness. Significantly, obedience helps to purify one's heart.

> But as he who called you is holy, so be holy in all you do; for it is written: "Be holy, because I am holy." (1 Peter 1:15–16 NIV)

> Seeing ye have purified your souls in obeying the truth through the Spirit unto unfeigned love of the brethren, see that ye love one another with a pure heart fervently. (1 Peter 1:22)

> Follow peace with all men, and holiness, without which no man shall see the Lord. (Hebrews12:14)

The twelfth chapter of Hebrews and the fourteenth verse says, "Without holiness we will not see the Lord." The scriptures also remind us that being peaceful with all men is a requisite of holiness. What is the relationship between peace and holiness? In order to understand the relationship, we must understand the definition of holiness. *Strong's Greek Lexicon*[16] uses the terms consecration, sanctification, and purification to interpret the Greek meaning of holiness. It is described as "the effect of consecration." It can be inferred from that definition that holiness is the state or quality of being set apart for the worship or service of God.

Holiness comes from a pure heart (Hebrews 2:14) that keeps itself from the defilement of sin and sinners. We cannot become holy without the Spirit of God. Galatians 5:22 tells us that the characteristics of holiness are found in the fruit of the Spirit: "love, joy, peace, longsuffering, kindness, goodness, faithfulness, gentleness, self-control. Against such there is no law." When we abide in Christ, through the anointing of the Holy Spirit, we bear fruit. One of them is the fruit of peace.

Spiritual maturity is a sign that one's life is built on faith.

After salvation, every believer begins the process of spiritual growth with the intent to become spiritually mature. God's promises are precious. Since we have these precious promises, we become partakers of the divine nature of God. This allows for us to escape the corruption of the world and enjoy the fruit of God's Word. This is where spiritual maturity begins. According to the apostle Paul, spiritual maturity is an ongoing process that will never end in this life.

Speaking of having the full knowledge of Christ, Paul tells us that he was not made perfect, but he would continue to press on to take hold of that which Christ Jesus had waiting for him. He said, "Brothers, I do not consider myself yet to have taken hold of it. But one thing I do: Forgetting what is behind and straining toward what is ahead, I press on toward the goal to win the prize for which God has called me heavenward in Christ Jesus." Just as Paul, the mature Christian, must press continually toward having a deeper knowledge of God in Christ, we must never be satisfied to the point that we stop growing. There is always more Word to supply our faith.

Christian maturity requires a thorough restructuring of one's priorities. We must work to please God, not selfishly obey our own impulses and desires. The key is to be consistent in our walk with Christ and to persevere in doing those things that we know will bring us closer to Him. This includes consistent practices of Bible reading/study, prayer, fellowship, service, and stewardship. However, no matter how hard we might work on those things, none of this is possible without the enabling of the Holy Spirit within us. Never stop striving and make every effort to reach forward by pressing onward to deeper spiritual qualities that will reinforce your faith. Do not stop swimming, or you will drift back. There is no floating in the Christian life.

Not as though I had already attained, either were already perfect: but I follow after if that I may apprehend that for which also I am apprehended of Christ Jesus. Brethren, I count not myself to have apprehended: but this one thing I do, forgetting those things which are behind, and reaching forth unto those things which are before, I press toward the mark for the prize of the high calling of God in Christ Jesus. (Philippians 3:12–14)

God's Word and the Mature Mind

Reading God's Word is a necessary requirement for spiritual growth. When we hide God's Word in our hearts, the Holy Spirit will bring the needed words to us at the right time. Each word is a truth that can sanctify the heart. Knowing the truth requires a commitment to follow righteousness: "Continue to work out your salvation with fear and trembling, for it is God who works in you to will and to act in order to fulfill his good purpose" (Philippians 2:12 NIV). This means that spiritual growth must be in alignment with the calling of the Holy Spirit in the heart. The believer must give the Holy Spirit authority to work with him, not just in him. The effort calls for seeking and obeying God with all your heart.

The mature believer rejoices in the truth of God and collaborates with the Holy Spirit as he is being led and guided into the truths of God's Word. The believer pursues God's truth and faithfully allows it to lead and guide into the promises of the Word. As we grow in grace and knowledge and obey God with our whole heart, our spirit grows as well (Acts 5:32).

The mature Christian is like a tree planted by a body of water.

The tree is compared to the matured Cristian who meditates in God's Word in the seventeenth chapter of Jeremiah, the eighth verse, and in the first chapter of Psalms, verses 1 through 3. Meditation is the source by which the Living Word of God comes into the heart and keeps the root system strong and sturdy. This makes the production of spiritual fruit possible.

> Blessed is the man that walketh not in the counsel of the ungodly, nor standeth in the way of sinners, nor sitteth in the seat of the scornful. But his delight is in the law of the Lord; and in his law doth he meditate day and night. And he shall be like a tree planted by the rivers of water, that bringeth forth his fruit in his season; his leaf also shall not wither; and whatsoever he doeth shall prosper. (Psalm1:1–3).

> Blessed is the man who trusts in the Lord, And whose hope is the Lord. For he shall be like a tree planted by the waters, Which spreads out its roots by the river, and will not fear when heat comes; But its leaf will be green, And will not be anxious in the year of drought, Nor will cease from yielding fruit. (Jeremiah 17:7– 8).

Fruit bearing is a process. The fruit does not just appear on a tree as soon as it is planted. A seed must be planted and sown for the plant to germinate and go through the maturing process. The same with a mature believer. The tree must mature before it can produce fruit. That is the law of seedtime and harvest.

> And God said, Let the earth bring forth grass, the herb yielding seed, and the fruit tree yielding fruit

after his kind, whose seed is in itself, upon the earth: and it was so. And the earth brought forth grass, and herb yielding seed after his kind, and the tree yielding fruit, whose seed was in itself, after his kind: and God saw that it was good. (Genesis 1:11–12)

Godly and Ungodly Fear

The person who fears the Lord loves reading the Word, and he is mightily blessed when he obeys it. God's words are His revelation of His will. The commandments of God are the revelation of His requirements. Spiritual faith in God's Word does the same thing as the natural soil does for the seed. It provides for growth reproduction and the bringing forth of spiritual fruit.

Godly Fear

The Bible commands us to fear God in the thirteenth chapter of Deuteronomy, the fourth verse. The believer who loves God and delights in His will operates in godly fear. This is fear that is holy and wise and will keep us from ungodly fear. It leads to holiness and righteous living. Paul speaks of this in the third chapter of Philippians, verses 12 through 14, when he tells us that he was not made perfect, but he would continue to press on to take hold of that which Christ Jesus had waiting for him. In specific, he said, "Brothers, I do not consider myself yet to have taken hold of it. But one thing I do: Forgetting what is behind and straining toward what is ahead, I press on toward the goal to win the prize for which God has called me heavenward in Christ Jesus." Just as Paul did, we must press continually toward deeper knowledge of God in Christ.

The fear of God is an acknowledgment that we know Him and are pleased to submit to His will for us.

> It is the Lord your God you must follow, and him you must revere. Keep his commands and obey him; serve him and hold fast to him. (Deuteronomy 13:4)

> Therefore, since we have these promises, dear friends, let us purify ourselves from everything that contaminates body and spirit, perfecting holiness out of reverence for God. (2 Corinthians 7:1)

Ungodly Fear

> For God hath not given us the spirit of fear; but of power, and of love, and of a sound mind. (2 Timothy 1:7)

It is normal for everyone to experience feelings of fear at times. In 2 Timothy 1:7, the Bible is not speaking of becoming afraid if you see something frightening. The Bible is speaking about a spirit of fear that dominates a person's life to the extent that they allow fear to rule over their lives and control their decisions. Fear and depression are closely related. The twenty-ninth chapter of Proverbs, verse 25, reads, "The fear of man bringeth a snare: but whoso putteth his trust in the LORD shall be safe." This means one fears the thoughts, opinions, and pressures of man more than God's commandments and laws. Fear causes an individual to compromise with sin. When faced with circumstances that go against the will of God, believers must be reminded of the fifth chapter of Acts, verse 29, which says, "We must obey God rather than men."

Love Casts Out Fear

> And we have known and believed the love that God
> hath to us. God is love; and he that dwelleth in love
> dwelleth in God, and God in him. Herein is our love
> made perfect, that we may have boldness in the day
> of judgment: because as he is, so are we in this world.
> There is no fear in love; but perfect love casteth out
> fear: because fear hath torment. He that feareth is
> not made perfect in love. We love him, because he
> first loved us. (1 John 4:16–19)

Fear was foreign to man until Adam sinned against God. When
Adam disobeyed God, he knew fear, hid from God, and said, "I
heard Your voice … I was afraid … I hid myself" (Genesis 3:10).
Since then, man has been living in the realm of fear. The Lord does
not want His people to be paralyzed by fear. First John 4:16–19
informs us that God is love, and He loves us. Anyone who "lives in
love lives in God, and God in them." We do not have to fear because
the Lord is on our side. He fights our battles. His love is made
complete in us. We can have confidence on the day of judgment. But
we are to be like Jesus while we are in the world. There is no fear
in love. And the one who fears is not made perfect in love. We can
remind ourselves that if we keep God's commandments and abide
in Him, we will abide in His love.

> "As the Father hath loved me, so have I loved you:
> continue ye in my love. If ye keep my commandments,
> ye shall abide in my love; even as I have kept my
> Father's commandments, and abide in his love.
> These things have I spoken unto you, that my joy
> might remain in you, and that your joy might be full.

This is my commandment, That ye love one another, as I have loved you. Greater love hath no man than this, that a man lay down his life for his friends. Ye are my friends, if ye do whatsoever I command you." (John 15: 9–14)

The Parable of the Mustard Seed

The purpose of every seed is to reproduce its own kind. Each seed has the potential to grow into a new, fully mature plant. In the same way, God is reproducing His own kind through man. As His "firstfruits," God gave us the "seed" of His Spirit, which leads and guides us into the truths of God's Word. Look at what Jesus had to say about the kingdom:

"So is the kingdom of God, as if a man should cast seed into the ground; And should sleep, and rise night and day, and the seed should spring and grow up, he knoweth not how. For the earth bringeth forth fruit of herself; first the blade, then the ear, after that the full corn in the ear. But when the fruit is brought forth, immediately he putteth in the sickle, because the harvest is come." (Mark 4:26–29)

The important meaning to draw from the mustard seed plant is that a huge and significant plant can come from a plant that started as a small, insignificant seed.

Then He said, "To what shall we liken the kingdom of God? Or with what parable shall we picture it? It is like a mustard seed which, when it is sown on the ground, is smaller than all the seeds on earth; but when it is sown, it grows up and becomes greater than all herbs, and shoots out large branches, so that the birds of the air may nest under its shade." (Mark 4:30–32 NKJV)

The little mustard seed is used in both Matthew and Luke to provide a picture of faith. This passage emphasizes the ability to "move mountains." The reference is to situations and circumstances in life that are difficult, frightening, disheartening, uncomfortable, or seemingly impossible. Those are conditions that it would seem only the supernatural power of God could overcome. Mustard seeds are exceedingly small. However, the plant that grows from the seed is large. Jesus's point is that faith can produce great results.

Parable of the Wheat and Tares

Tares are the weeds that grow with the good seed. Weeds grow and choke the other plants. This leaves the good plants extraordinarily little space to grow. Weeds work in the lives of Christians in the same way. They crowd and distract to prevent spiritual growth and worship of God. We can surmise from the parable of the sower that when left unchecked, weeds in our lives can choke and prevent us from living fruitful lives.

> Another parable He put forth to them, saying: "The kingdom of heaven is like a man who sowed good seed in his field; but while men slept, his enemy came and sowed tares among the wheat and went his way. But when the grain had sprouted and produced a crop, then the tares also appeared. So the servants of the owner came and said to him, 'Sir, did you not

so good seed in your field? How then does it have tares?' He said to them, 'An enemy has done this.' The servants said to him, 'Do you want us then to go and gather them up?' But he said, 'No, lest while you gather up the tares you also uproot the wheat with them. Let both grow together until the harvest, and at the time of harvest I will say to the reapers, "First gather together the tares and bind them in bundles to burn them, but gather the wheat into my barn." (Matthew13:24–30)

The Parable of the Tares Explained

Then Jesus sent the multitude away and went into the house. And His disciples came to Him, saying, "Explain to us the parable of the tares of the field." He answered and said to them: "He who sows the good seed is the Son of Man. The field is the world, the good seeds are the sons of the kingdom, but the tares are the sons of the wicked one. The enemy who sowed them is the devil, the harvest is the end of the age, and the reapers are the angels. Therefore as the tares are gathered and burned in the fire, so it will be at the end of this age. The Son of Man will send out His angels, and they will gather out of His kingdom all things that offend, and those who practice lawlessness, and will cast them into the furnace of fire. There will be wailing and gnashing of teeth. Then the righteous will shine forth as the sun in the kingdom of their Father. He who has ears to hear, let him hear!" (Matthew 24:30–43)

Present-Day Meaning of the Parable of the Wheat and Tares

The church is a place where people with diverse levels of spiritual growth abide together. The parable reveals what Satan tries to do to the church. It also gives insight into who comes to church. God plants good seeds that become His kingdom children. Satan, the wicked one, plants those who are his. The faithful live to please and acknowledge God through obedience.

Revelation Knowledge, Wisdom, and Understanding

Spiritual growth is a mystery that involves the growth of the Word of God (Word Seed) in the life of the believer. Just as natural seeds follow the processes of germination, development, transitions, fruition, and multiplication in the life of plants, the seed of God's Word follows the same process in the lives of Christians.

Jesus used the seed as a metaphor to show the life of the kingdom sown into the soil of people's hearts (Matthew13:4) and for the sowing of the children of the kingdom into the world (Matthew 13:38). Peter helps us to understand that seed is life that is provided for believers when they receive the Word of God in (1 Peter 1:23). Paul uses seed in the same way when he says, "I planted the seed, Apollos watered it, but God made it grow" (1 Corinthians 3:6). Crops are produced when seeds are planted. They produce harvests. This involves both conformation and transformation.

> Being born again, not of corruptible seed, but of incorruptible, by the word of God, which liveth and abideth for-ever. (1 Peter 1:23)

"Verily, verily, I say unto you, Except a corn of wheat fall into the ground and die, it abideth alone: but if it die, it bringeth forth much fruit." (John 12:24)

Strong's Greek Lexicon [17] defines revelation from its root word "reveal," which means to manifest; to unveil; to uncover; to open. It is the work of the Holy Spirit to reveal the knowledge of God to Christians. In fact, it is the work of the Holy Spirit to reveal the meaning of all truth to the Christian. This is clearly seen in 1 Corinthians 1:9–16 where the wisdom of the world is contrasted with the wisdom of God. A spiritual Christian sees (through the Spirit revealing to him) the meaning behind world events as well as day-to-day experiences. He understands who and what are behind the events of history and human experience. Therefore, he gains a growing knowledge of God and the revelation of the seed parables.

"But the Comforter, which is the Holy Ghost, whom the Father will send in my name, he shall teach you all things, and bring all things to your remembrance, whatsoever I have said unto you." (John 14:26)

"I have yet many things to say unto you, but ye cannot bear them now. Howbeit when he, the Spirit of truth, is come, he will guide you into all truth: for he shall not speak of himself; but whatsoever he shall hear, that shall he speak: and he will shew you things to come. He shall glorify me: for he shall receive of mine, and shall shew it unto you. All things that the Father hath are mine: therefore said I, that he shall take of mine, and shall shew it unto you." (John 16:12–15)

Transforming the Heart

> But we all, with open face beholding as in a glass the
> glory of the Lord, are changed into the same image
> from glory to glory, even as by the Spirit of the Lord.
> (2 Corinthians 3:18)

In 2 Corinthians 3:18, Paul speaks of the Christian's being "transformed into the same image from glory to glory." This passage reveals the Word as a mirror in which the glory of Christ has the ability to be reflected in the lives of Christians. When Christians study the Word of God, their lives become transformed into God's likeness. His glory becomes their glory. His life becomes their reflection.

> Knowing this, that our old man is crucified with
> [him], that the body of sin might be destroyed, that
> henceforth we should not serve sin. (Romans 6:6)

The "old man" is referred to as the flesh or the old nature. It is the "old self" or the nature that we had before we were born again. The old nature (flesh) is characterized by evil desires, bondage to sin, and love of sin. It is the sinful nature that we received from Adam. Significantly, the old man or nature is opposed to the things of God.

> And have put on the new [man], which is renewed in
> knowledge after the image of him that created him.
> (Colossians 3:10)

> I am crucified with Christ, nevertheless I live, yet
> not I, but Christ liveth in me; and the life which I
> now live in the flesh I live by the faith of the Son

of God, Who loved me and gave Himself for me.
(Galatians 2:20)

To be crucified means to die. We must continually die to self
and from sin. The old nature or that inborn tendency to sin was
crucified with Christ. The work of the Holy Spirit and our faith
and trust in the Word of God assist us in reckoning ourselves to be
dead to the old sinful nature and its lusts. This means that we do
not live under the influence of the power of sin but choose instead
to live for God. The Word reinforces this belief in Colossians 3:10
and Galatians 2:20.

It is important that we remain anchored and steadfast in life; we
must also commit ourselves to the fellowship that is provided from
the Word of God and communion with God. Likewise, if we are to
be followers of Christ, we will have a foundation that is built upon
faith in the Word and obedience to its commands. Sequentially, we
will receive wisdom, strength, and guidance to live peaceful and
prosperous lives, no matter what the circumstances.

WAITING

Key scripture: "But they who wait for the Lord shall renew their strength; they shall mount up with wings like eagles; they shall run and not be weary; they shall walk and not faint" (Isaiah 40:30–31).

The Seed of the Word

The key to understanding what today's key scripture means is to know what the word, *Wait,* means. *Wait* is a Hebrew word. *The Blue Book Bible's International Standard Bible Dictionary*[18] defines its meaning: "to bind together like a cord (rope with many strands)." Just as a rope's strength comes from having many strands, so our strength comes through being tightly united in a relation with the Father, Son, and Holy Spirit. The more strands that we weave into our relationship with the Lord, the more strength He gives to us. Praying, reading the Bible, listening to teaching and preaching, and fellowshipping with God are personal activities that we must do. No one can do them for us. When we do those things, we exchange our strength for the Lord's strength and meet challenges as if we have powerful wings like an eagle. Importantly, we can run through life and not be weary and walk through problems and not faint.

The Action of the Word

Many believers struggle with two problems: Why doesn't God answer my prayer sometimes? Why does God allow the evil to prosper while the righteous suffer? While going through a tumultuous situation, the prophet Habakkuk asked the Lord the following question: "O Lord, how long shall I cry for help, and you will not hear?" The Bible says the Lord finally answered him (Habakkuk 1:5). The Lord's answer was "Look among the nations, and see; wonder and be astounded. For I am doing a work in your days that you would not believe if told" (verse 5). God is omnipotent, omniscient, and omnipresent. He is all-powerful, in control, and can handle any problems we face. He is an all-knowing God and knows every detail of our lives—from our birth to our death. Importantly, we will meet every situation that we will face. Nothing surprises him or leaves him unsure of how to work things for our good. That is because He is omnipresent (all-present) and always with us, even when we feel alone.

The Persistence of the Word

Our faith is often tested during the many difficult circumstances of life. It is during long and painful seasons where endurance, or trustingly waiting for the Lord to act, becomes primary in our lives. "The Lord is good to those who wait for Him" (Lamentations 3:25). He also promises to give us what we need to endure (Isaiah 40:30–31); and to hear us when speak to Him (Micah 7:7). We need to wait with confidence for the Lord to act on our behalf, knowing that His promises are "yes,' and "amen' in Christ Jesus (2 Corinthians 1:20).

What Is the Word Saying to You?

TEMPTATIONS AND CONDEMNATION

Key scripture: "Therefore let him who thinks he stands take heed lest he fall. No temptation has overtaken you except such as is common to man; but God is faithful, who will not allow you to be tempted beyond what you are able, but with the temptation will also make the way of escape, that you may be able to bear it" (1 Corinthians 10:12–13).

The Seed of the Word

No one is immune to sin just because he/she is saved. As a matter of fact, temptation (enticement to sin) is a part of life. At times, the power to commit sin seems stronger than the desire to resist. However, Christians are saved by grace through faith in Christ. We can walk in the Spirit and resist sin, or we can live our life in the lust of the flesh and commit sin. God promises us that we can "Resist the Devil and he will flee from you" (James 4:7). And no temptation is irresistible. You can trust God to keep the temptation from becoming so strong that you cannot stand up against it, for He has promised this and will do what He says. He will show you how to escape temptation's power so that you can bear up patiently against it (NLT).

The Action of the Word

Condemnation is a feeling of guilt, shame, fear, and unworthiness that comes when we cannot seem to forgive ourselves for something we have done in the past or just recently. Jesus paid the ultimate price for us to be free from sin and condemnation. That means that when you became a Christian, you became a new creation. The old person died, spiritually speaking. And all our past and future mistakes have been blotted out by the blood of Jesus! If Jesus can forgive you for past and future sins, you must forgive yourself. Importantly, when you sin or miss the mark; confess and repent as soon as you realize it. For, "If we confess our sins to Him, He is faithful and just to forgive us and cleanse us from all unrighteousness" (1 John 1:9).

The Persistence of the Word

God hates sin (Proverbs 6:16–19). And Jesus not only died for our sins; He took them upon Himself so He could give us His righteousness. This means that we are saved and declared righteous because of what Christ has done for us (justification). After we are saved, we begin an ongoing process of sanctification of being conformed to God's image and becoming more like Christ. Allowing the Holy Spirit to convict us of sin, which leads to godly sorrow, confession of sin, and heartfelt repentance, plays an important role in sanctification.

What Is This Word Saying to You?

HEARING FROM GOD

Key scripture: "The secret of the Lord is with them that fear him; and he will shew them his covenant" (Psalm 25:14).

The Seed of the Word

Job 28:28 reads, "Behold, the fear of the Lord, that is wisdom; and to depart from evil is understanding." Jesus Christ is the wisdom of God. His Word is His Covenant. James 1:5 tells us how to find wisdom, "If any of you lacks wisdom, let him ask God, who gives generously to all without reproach, and it will be given him." We can pray to receive wisdom and revelation knowledge from the Lord (Ephesians 1:17). Jesus sent His Holy Spirit to lead and guide us into all truths. Through prayer, meditation on the Word of God, fellowshipping with the people of God, and worship, we make ourselves constantly available to hear from God.

The Action of the Word

One of the greatest benefits of being a Christian is to be able to hear God speak to us personally. The Lord speaks to us and gives us directions constantly. Most of the time, we do not know when He speaks because we are not discerning that He is speaking. Therefore, we do not hear Him. To hear God when He speaks to us, we must have a discernment of how He speaks and communicates with us on a personal level. Romans 12:2 reads, "Do not conform to the pattern of this world but be transformed by the renewing of your mind. Then you will be able to test and approve what God's will is—his good, pleasing, and perfect will." This requires knowing the Lord through prayer, fellowship, reading, and meditating on His Word.

The Persistence of the Word

Revelation knowledge occur when the knowledge of God's Word enters our minds and causes our spirits to bear witness with the truth of God's Word, through hearing or studying it. Revelation knowledge comes with wisdom, which is the ability to apply knowledge. The Holy Spirit is the source of revelation knowledge. Most of the time, we do not know when He speaks; therefore, we do not hear Him. To hear God when He speaks to us, we must have a discernment of how He speaks and communicates with us on a personal level, taking time to speak to Him and listen for His answer. He is available to speak to the hearts of all who put their trust in Jesus Christ. The Holy Spirit has been described as a gift (Acts 2:38), a wind (John 3:8), and a dove (Mark 1:10). He is the Spirit of God who is always present to hear from you.

What Is This Word Saying to You?

PRAYER AND DEPENDENCE ON GOD

Key scripture: "If my people, who are called by my name, will humble themselves and pray and seek my face and turn from their wicked ways, then I will hear from heaven, and I will forgive their sin and will heal their land" (2 Chronicles 7:14).

Seed of the Word

After he had built and dedicated the Temple to God, King Solomon prayed for God's blessings and favor on His people and on the Temple (read the second chapter of 2 Chronicles). God responded to him by saying, "I have heard your prayer and have chosen this place for myself … When I shut up the heavens so that there is no rain, or command locusts to devour the land or send a plague among my people, if my people, who are called by my name, will humble themselves and pray and seek my face and turn from their wicked ways, then will I hear from heaven and will forgive their sin and will heal their land" (verses 13–14 of chapter 7). God knows that His people will face wars, pandemics, and other catastrophic events, in addition to dealing with our own individual concerns. The Word says that if we humble ourselves and pray and turn from our ways, God will hear us from heaven and heal our land. Given the circumstances in current events, this verse becomes even more powerful.

Action of the Word

We can find accounts of the prophet Elijah's life in 1 Kings 17–19 and 2 Kings 1–2. His prayers were powerful and effective because he learned to be completely dependent on God. When we read the accounts of his life, we find that at times he seemed to have incredible faith in God. However, at other times, he seemed fearful and uncertain. Elijah learned to pray, listen to God's voice, and walk in obedience to His Word. As a result, he performed many miraculous and amazing things in his life. Spending time with God in prayer helps us to be attentive to His voice. If we are obedient and yield to His Word, we position ourselves to live righteous lives and see answers to our prayers.

Persistence of the Word

Do not be anxious about anything, but in every situation, by prayer and petition, with thanksgiving, present your requests to God. (Philippians 4:6)

There is a simple message here: "Do not worry about anything and give all of your cares to God." This does not mean that we should not be concerned about what happens to us and our loved ones; nor does it mean that we are to be careless and unconcerned about life. It means that we should not be fearful, paranoid, anxious, stressed, or uneasy about our lives and circumstances. Instead, we are to spend time praying directly to God, who is the Creator and maker of heaven and earth. He has all power and authority and is in total control of every situation.

What Is This Word Saying to You?

SPIRITUAL BATTLE AND SPIRITUAL WEAPONS

Key scripture: "No weapon formed against you shall prosper, and every tongue which rises against you in judgment You shall condemn. This is the heritage of the servants of the Lord, and their righteousness is from Me, Says the Lord" (Isaiah 54:17).

The Seed of the Word

The word *prosper* in this scripture means "to succeed." In the book of Isaiah, God promised the people of Jerusalem that no enemy will be able to have final and ultimate prosperity over them. The tactics of the enemy against God's people may appear to prosper for a time, but there will never be final success. God is in control of our lives. He controls those who make weapons and those who use them. Even when bad things happen to us—when we feel defeated and crushed by our enemies—we can trust and not be afraid because "God is our shelter and strength, always ready to help in times of trouble" (Psalm 46:1). Believers must learn to make use of the shield of faith, "with which you can extinguish all the flaming arrows of the evil one" (Ephesians 6:16). No matter what the devil creates to throw at us, it will fail in the end because God is the sovereign ruler of our destiny.

The Action of the Word

Word Seed: "For though we walk in the flesh, we do not war according to the flesh. For the weapons of our warfare are not carnal but mighty in God for pulling down strongholds." (2 Corinthians 10:3–4).

Many of the battles that we fight daily are spiritual ones. They come from the powers of darkness that are all around us. Apart from the power of God, all of our energies combined are to no avail against the power of darkness. We need spiritual weapons to fight spiritual battles. Prayer and the Word of God are spiritual weapons (Ephesians 6:17–18). Importantly, we have all of God's spiritual armor to protect us (Ephesians 6:10–18). Jesus Christ has defeated the final enemy, who is death, and purchased for us eternal life (2 Timothy 1:10). He will protect and uphold us, no matter what we face. He will also and help us through to the final victory (Isaiah 41:10). This is our heritage as "servants of the LORD" (Isaiah 54:17b).

The Persistence of the Word

We need spiritual weapons to fight the battles in our lives. However, the Lord has given us His Word as our sword and faith as our shield (Hebrews 4:12). We have His spiritual armor to protect us (Ephesians 6:10–18). Jesus Christ has defeated the final enemy, who is death, and purchased for us eternal life (2 Timothy 1:10). He will protect and uphold His children, no matter what we face, and help us through to the final victory (Isaiah 41:10). "'This is the heritage of the servants of the LORD, and their righteousness is from Me,' Says the LORD" (Isaiah 54:17b).

What Is This Word Saying to You?

THE LORD IS ACQUAINTED
WITH OUR HEARTS

Key scripture: "Keep (Guard) your heart with all vigilance, for from it flow the springs of life" (Proverbs 4:23).

The Seed of the Word

The heart is valuable. It is not only valuable; it is connected to God. God works with us by teaching us to change the thought process through the way we think about things. As we read the Word of God, our minds are continuously renewed and transformed (Romans 12:2). The key scripture for today is summarized by the scriptures that come before and after it: "My child, pay attention to what I say. Listen carefully to my words. Do not lose sight of them. Let them penetrate deep into your heart, for they bring life to those who find them, and healing to their whole body. Avoid all perverse talk; stay away from corrupt speech. Look straight ahead and fix your eyes on what lies before you. Mark out a straight path for your feet; stay on the safe path. Don't get sidetracked; keep your feet from following evil" (Proverbs 4:20–22, 24–27).

The Action of the Word

O lord, thou hast searched me, and known me. Whither shall I go from thy spirit? or whither shall I flee from thy presence? (Psalm19:1, 7)

The Lord God is Almighty, omniscient, omnipotent, and omnipresent. He knows all about each one of us and is interested in the smallest detail of our lives. Importantly, He searches out each thought of our heart, knows every deep longing within us, is acquainted with all our ways, and understands the deepest thoughts of our innermost being. He is also our salvation and the only source of grace, truth, mercy, love, peace, and hope.

The Persistence of the Word

A man's heart plans his way, But the Lord directs his steps. (Proverbs 16:9)

All of us have hopes and dreams for certain things to happen in our lives, and when they do not happen when we think they should, we become frustrated. Much of that frustration may be alleviated when we understand that the Lord orders man's steps or ways (Psalm 37:23). He directs our paths and does not always allow us to see the exact timing of His plan. We must learn to trust our lives to His care. The sooner we understand and accept that, the sooner God can work His plan in our lives.

What Is This Word Saying to You?

ABIDING AND FRUIT BEARING

Key scripture: "Abide in Me, and I in you. As the branch cannot bear fruit of itself, unless it abides in the vine, neither can you, unless you abide in Me. I am the vine; you are the branches. He who abides in Me, and I in him, bears much fruit; for without Me you can do nothing." (John 15:4–5 NKJV)

The Seed of the Word

Being fruitful means to be connected to Christ. Just as a vine's branches rely on being connected to the trunk from which they receive their energy to bear fruit, believers must depend on being connected to Christ for their spiritual life and the ability to grow into spiritual maturity. The source of life is found in Him. When we are connected to the vine, the fruit that we produce begins to produce more fruit: "love, joy, peace, patience, goodness, kindness, gentleness, faithfulness, and self-control" (Galatians 5:22–23).

The Action of the Word

Word Seed: "For it is God who works in you to will and to act in order to fulfill his good purpose" (Philippians 2:13).

It is important to understand that being fruitful is accomplished by the Holy Spirit working in and through the believer, not through mere human willpower. "For we are his workmanship, created in Christ Jesus unto good works, which God hath before ordained that we should walk in them" (Ephesians 2:10). The Lord does not compel or force us against our will. He leads us to will as well as to do. This leads to life where love, joy, peace, patience, kindness, goodness, faithfulness, gentleness, and self-control are demonstrated.

The Persistence of the Word

Being fruitful requires not just an ongoing relationship with Christ but one that is continually deepening and expanding (Hebrews 6:1). "For it is God who works in you to will and to act in order to fulfill his good purpose" (Philippians 2:13). It is important to understand that being fruitful is accomplished by the Holy Spirit working in and through the believer, not through mere human willpower. So what does this fruit look like? Good fruit is seen in a change in our disposition, attitudes, affections, and actions. Those sins that we formerly loved start to become loathsome to us (Romans 6:21). We begin to love others with the love of Christ.

What Is This Word Saying to You?

OVERCOMING LIFE'S CHALLENGES

Word Seed: "These things I have spoken unto you, that in me ye might have peace. In the world ye shall have tribulation: but be of good cheer; I have overcome the world" (John 16:33).

The Seed of the Word

The Christian life is a life of warfare. We are called to be good soldiers of the Lord Jesus Christ and "to war a good warfare" (1 Timothy 1:18). The Bible says, "In all these things we are more than conquerors through him who loved us" (Romans 8:37). The word for conqueror is the same word for overcomer. We are more than conquerors because Christ conquered (and obtained victory over) sin, death, and the devil. Due to Christ, we do not have to fight. We simply stand on the victory that He accomplished on our behalf. Do not allow circumstances to move you; put on God's armor (Ephesians 6:10–18), fight with your faith, contend with prayers, and your victory is sure.

The Action of the Word

Spiritual warfare for the Christian is less about worrying about problems and fighting our enemies and more about believing that Jesus is Lord over whatever situations we face. Unbelief says we must contend with the enemy and fight for the victory, but faith says that Jesus has already won our battles. Believe that you are an overcomer! Your victory will come when you start having faith in what God's Word says about you.

The Persistence of the Word

If we are going rise above hardships, finish the course, endure until the end, and sit down with Jesus on the throne, we must overcome the challenges that invade our Christian walk. We all know that we will face hardship, turmoil, and tragedy. However, it is our reaction to those challenges that will determine if we are overcomers. We will face a lot of battles in life, but we must always keep in mind that God has a plan for good for each of us. In our personal relationships, the Word of God tells us to overcome evil with good (Romans 12:21). As you put your focus on Him as your indicator, it becomes easier and easier to walk in peace.

What Is the Word Saying to You?

LOVE IS IMPORTANT

Key scripture: "Dear friends, let us love one another, for love comes from God. Everyone who loves has been born of God and knows God. Whoever does not love does not know God, because God is love" (1 John 4:7).

The Seed of Love

The Bible teaches us that "God is love." He is our perfect example of how to love others. God's love is referred to as agape love, which is the highest form of love. His love is generous, unselfish, self-sacrificing, sacrificial, steadfast, unchanging, and unconditional. The Bible teaches believers that the world will know us by our love (John 13:35). The greatest testimony that we can be is to love those around us, whether family, friends, or strangers.

The Action of Love

> Though I speak with the tongues of men and of angels, and have not charity, I am become as sounding brass, or a tinkling cymbal. And though I have the gift of prophecy, and understand all mysteries, and all knowledge; and though I have all faith, so that I could remove mountains, and have not charity, I am nothing. (1 Corinthians 13:1–3)

This Word speaks to all of us. It does this by showing us that outside of love, anything that we do is noise and has no spiritual value. That is because God is love (1 John 4:7), and any action of love is a representation of His presence. Spiritual gifts are a wonderful blessing from God, but compared to the value of love, they are nothing. Those who have received spiritual gifts must use them in love, patience, and kindness.

The Persistence of Love

> Love suffers long and is kind; love does not envy; love does not parade itself, is not puffed up; does not behave rudely, does not seek its own, is not provoked, thinks no evil; does not rejoice in iniquity, but rejoices in the truth; bears all things, believes all things, hopes all things, endures all things. (1 Corinthians 13:4–7)

Chapter 13 of 1 Corinthians tells us what love means and shows us how God wants us to walk in love. This chapter shows us that without love, everything that we do is meaningless. The word *love* is translated from the Greek word *agape*.[19] Agape love leads to actions and sacrifice on the behalf of others. To "suffer long," behave properly, live selfless lives, live temperate lives, and have love for one another, we must allow the fruit-bearing Holy Spirit to release faith in our lives so that we can be transformed daily into the image of Jesus Christ. Then we will be able to endure those things that we previously thought were impossible.

What Is This Word Saying to You?

STANDING IN THE GAP

Key scripture: "I looked for someone among them who would build up the wall and stand before me in the gap on behalf of the land so I would not have to destroy it, but I found no one" (Ezekiel 22:30).

The Seed of the Word

We read in the Bible where tall walls surrounded cites to provide protection from enemies. There were times when the walls needed mending or simply had not been completed, exposing occupants to the assaults and dangers of their enemies. In many instances, people had to risk their lives by' "standing in the gap" between walls to fight the enemy. The key scripture revealed the need of prophets, kings, priests, apostles, and called men of God to intercede on behalf of the people, or to stand in the gap to be advocates for them. The conclusion was that He could not find anyone.

The Action of the Word

The most prominent example of one standing in the gap before God was our Lord and Savior Jesus Christ. His very purpose for coming to earth as a man was to give His life as an atoning sacrifice for the sins of the entire human race. This was the ultimate act of standing in the gap to recompense for God's judgment. Sin left man vulnerable to divine punishment, but Jesus willingly offered His life as the only acceptable payment for that sin when He stood in the gap by hanging on the cross of Calvary and dying for us. The Lord is looking for men and woman to intercede with Him on behalf of the world and His sinful people today.

The Persistence of the Word

Jesus said, "By this all shall know that you are My disciples, if you have love toward one another" (John 13:35). We can show our love for the world by praying for one another and for those who do not know Christ as Savior. This may include praying against the enemies of God's people, praying for communities and nations, and praying for those living in sin and disobedience.

What Is This Word Saying to You?

SALT AND LIGHT

Key scriptures: "You are the light of the world. A town built on a hill cannot be hidden. Neither do people light a lamp and put it under a bowl. Instead, they put it on its stand, and it gives light to everyone in the house. In the same way, let your light shine before others, that they may see your good deeds and glorify your Father in heaven" (Matthew 5:14–16).

"You are the salt of the earth; but if the salt loses its flavor, how shall it be seasoned? It is then good for nothing but to be thrown out and trampled underfoot by men. You are the light of the world. A city that is set on a hill cannot be hidden" (Matthew 5:13–14).

The Seed of the Word

Light is used to symbolize God, faith, or holiness throughout scripture. As Christians are enlightened by the truth of the Savior and His love for all humankind, they should become living representatives of Him. A city set in the heights has the advantage of seeing the surrounding territory from some distance, but this also means that people in the surrounding territory can always see the city as well. One cannot hide a city on a hill! As light shines in darkness, so our faith must be evident to all men.

Salt is a seasoner and preserver of foods. It is also used to make leather, pottery, and other chemical products. More than half of the chemical products we make use salt. Salt is a universal cleanser. It can remove toxic substances and cleanse the body. We spread it across roads and streets in places where it snows. Jesus identifies salt with fire and living at peace collectively in Mark 9:49–50.

The Action of the Word

God has called believers out of the world to proclaim the "marvelous light," and that light is Jesus Christ (John 8:12). We can be a light to the world, but Jesus is the Light of the World (John 9:5). Only light can overcome darkness (John 1:5). We cannot overcome anything of ourselves. The point is that only by the blood of the Lamb of God do we overcome (Revelation 12:11).

The Persistence of the Word

God calls every Christian to influence the world and those around them. This is equivalent to being salt and light. Salt is a stabilizing substance and works only when it is not contaminated by other chemicals. To be salt means to seek to influence people by showing them the unconditional love of Christ through good deeds. Light illuminates and penetrates darkness. To be light means to be a witness to others concerning the truth of God's Word.

What Is This Word Saying to You?

WISDOM, KNOWLEDGE, AND UNDERSTANDING

Key scripture: "By wisdom a house is built, and by understanding it is established; by knowledge the rooms are filled with all precious and pleasant riches" (Proverbs 24:3–4).

The Seed of the Word

The word *house* is a symbol of a person, a family, or a home. God never intended for believers to walk through the world alone. Our lives must be established on His Word and built by the wisdom that comes only from Him. Psalm 127:1 says, "Unless the Lord builds the house, they labor in vain who build it." God never intended you to walk through the Word and walk through the world alone. If the Lord is not the builder of our lives, our foundations will crack. If our lives are built with wisdom, knowledge, and understanding from God, the Holy Spirit will show us every area in our lives that needs attention.

The Action of the Word

The fear of the Lord is different from fear of accidents, disease, war, famine, death, and other concerns. Fearing God is knowing that we do not give account to anyone but God for our actions. If we do not fear God, we will not take sin seriously. The consequences of sin are enormous. It is true that God is full of grace and long-suffering. But even when we have been forgiven for our sins, we still must reap the results of having committed them (Galatians 6:7–8). When we consider our words and actions on the scale of godly fear, we gain wisdom and understanding.

The Persistence of the Word

Wisdom, knowledge, and understanding are qualities believers need in order to know what to do in given situations. Believers with knowledge *know* the scriptures. God's Word is literally in them. However, it is possible to have knowledge of what is in the Word of God but lack understanding (have no clue of the meaning of what they read or what to do next). With understanding, one is able to comprehend meaning from the scriptures they read. Those with wisdom know which principle to apply, what to do next, and what direction to go. As we read God's Word, we will receive His wisdom, knowledge, and understanding about any issue that we desire to know. James 1:5 tells us that if you ask for wisdom, God will give it generously without finding fault.

What Is This Word Saying to You?

GUIDANCE

Key scripture: "And you shall know the truth, and the truth shall make you free" (John 8:32).

The Seed of the Word

Truth in this passage means knowledge grounded in personal experience. Jesus asked the Father to sanctify the believer by His truth. He continued to say, "Your word is truth" (John 17:17). The meaning of the word *sanctify* in this passage is "separation (set a-part)." Sanctification is the process by which believers are to be shaped or transformed into Christ's image. It is only through the continuous study of God's Word that one learns and can therefore emulate the "mind of Christ" (1 Corinthians 2:16).

The Action of the Word

"Receive with meekness the implanted Word, which is able to save your souls." (James 1:21b)

Our physical bodies consist of many types of substances, but the foremost substance needed for survival is food. Without eating, we cannot continue to exist. In the same way, for the believer to be healthy and live the abundant life, the Word of God (spiritual food) is needed. We continue to live in a state of defeat until we die to self and allow the Word of God, through the Holy Spirit, to have full control of our lives. God's words refresh our minds, hearts, and souls. It is a "light unto the path" of the soul (Psalm 119:105). It is also "a mirror" that shows us our soul as it really is (James 1:23). Importantly, it revives the soul (Psalm19:7) and introduces us to the one who is the "living word."

The Persistence of the Word

Jesus spoke the following to believers: "If you continue or abide in my word, then are ye my disciples indeed, and ye shall know the truth, and the truth shall make you free" (John 8:31–32). Continuing in the Word means one must not only hear the Word of God but continue to be led by the Holy Spirit after receiving it. Feelings have no place in the search for the truth of God's Word. Belief moves one to accept God's Word, receive it, and then obey it. In other words, you will struggle with truth before you understand the full joy of God's grace. A primary reason that God gave the Bible is found in 2 Timothy 3:16, which helps to understand that the Word of God is inspired by Him, and is useful for doctrine, reproof, correction, and righteous teaching. When one allows the Word to lead and guide his actions, he becomes perfect (mature, complete, having reached its end).

What Is This Word Saying to You?

THE LORD IS MY LIFE

Key scripture: "The LORD is my strength and song and is become my salvation" (Psalm 118:14).

The Seed of the Word

The sovereignty of Jesus is found throughout the Bible. He came from heaven to earth, was born of a virgin in Bethlehem, lived a perfect life, died a sacrificial death, was buried in a tomb, was raised victoriously, and ascended into heaven to occupy His throne in glory, where "God has highly exalted Him and given Him the name which is above every name." As Lord, He is the ruler, the commander, and the master of our whole lives. He cannot be part Lord. He must be given the entire control of our lives. "Therefore God has highly exalted Him and given Him the name, which is above every name, that at the name of Jesus every knee should bow, of those in heaven and those on earth, and of those under the earth, and that every tongue should confess that Jesus Christ is Lord, to the glory of God the Father" (Philippians 2:9–11 NKJV).

The Action of the Word

While Jesus Christ was always God the Son, He had to pass the test of obedience while he lived in the body of a human being. He had to and did live a sinless life amid every form of temptation (Hebrews 4:14–16). As a result of His fulfilled mission on earth, God the Father named Jesus Lord, to His glory. As God's children, adopted into His family, we have been assured an inheritance from our heavenly Father. "Now if we are children, then we are heirs—heirs of God and co-heirs with Christ, if indeed we share in his sufferings in order that we may also share in his glory" (Romans 8:17). Christ's life is the light that overcame darkness to be our salvation: "In him was life, and the life was the light of men. As Sons of God, and joint heirs with Jesus, we share in the inheritance of Jesus. Everything that belongs to Him belong to us: His glory (John 17:22), His riches (2 Corinthians 8:9), His sufferings (1 Peter 4:13), and all things (Hebrews 1:2).

The Persistence of the Word

Jesus not only died for our sin, but after this death on the cross, He physically came back to life three days later, just as He said He would. This was final proof that everything that He said about Himself was true. And He now invites us to come to Him, that we might begin a personal relationship with God. We do not come to make Jesus Lord. He is Lord! Our responsibility is to submit to His lordship by yielding to His will and His Word by allowing the power of the Holy spirit to lead and guide us into all truth (John 14:16–17). "For if we live, we live to the Lord; and if we die, we die to the Lord. Therefore, whether we live or die, we are the Lord's. For to this end Christ died, and rose and lived again, that he might be Lord of both the dead and the living" (Romans 14:8–9 NKJV).

What Is the Word Saying to You?

JESUS IS LORD!

Word Seed: "God has made this Jesus, whom you crucified, both Lord and Messiah" (Acts 2:36b).

The Seed of the Word

There is a day coming when every person who has ever lived will bow and acknowledge that Jesus Christ is King of kings and Lord of lords (Philippians 2:9–11). Romans 10:9 shows that this personal confirmation is required for the salvation of all: "if you confess with your mouth that Jesus is Lord and believe in your heart that God raised him from the dead, you will be saved." We have been bought with a price by the sacrifice of Christ (1 Corinthians 6:20). If you genuinely believe and trust this in your heart, receiving Jesus alone as your Savior, declaring, "Jesus is Lord," you will be saved from judgment and spend eternity with God in heaven.

The Action of the Word

When we accept Jesus Christ as our Savior, we cannot and do not receive Him as Savior only. We receive Him as Lord and Savior. "For in Him we live and move and have our being" (Acts 17:28). The statement "Jesus is Lord" indicates that Jesus is the Son of God. He holds "all authority in heaven and on earth" (Matthew 28:18). He is "Lord of the Sabbath" (Luke 6:5); "our only Sovereign and Lord" (Jude 1:4); and "the Lord of lords" (Revelation 17:14). We have all sinned and deserve God's judgment. My appeal to all is to make Jesus Christ your Lord and master.

The Persistence of the Word

By His grace, God has already purchased salvation, healing, deliverance, provision, and peace through the blood of His beloved Son, Jesus Christ. When Christ is the priority, we get everything else we need. Not only that, but He provides rest. Through His death, Jesus made sure that we have everything we need to succeed in life (2 Peter 1:3). His glory and excellence have given us great and precious promises. These are the promises that enable you to share His divine nature and escape the world's corruption caused by human desires (2 Peter 1:3–4).

What Is This Word Saying to You?

THE GOD-CENTERED LIFE

Word Seed: "Love not the world, neither the things that are in the world. If any man loves the world, the love of the Father is not in him" (1 John 2:15).

The Seed of the Word

We cannot love both the world and the Father at the same time. Loving the world means being faithful to the world's values and philosophies. It also means focusing on things you can see, touch, and feel, such as food, drink, leisure, sex, rest, enjoyment, comfort, and others. Those are the things that appeal to how you feel in the body. What we love is always about what we desire in our hearts. Loving the things of the world never satisfies the longing of the heart. The Lord is the only one who can satisfy the heart. "For all that is in the world—the desires of the flesh and the desires of the eyes and pride of life—is not from the Father but is from the world. And the world is passing away along with its desires, but whoever does the will of God abides forever" (1 John 2:16–17).

The Action of the Word

Jesus Christ is the Lamb of God. He is the rock of our salvation and the light of the world (John 1:29, John 8:12). He is the bread of life, the true vine, and the Good Shepherd (John 6:35, John 15:1, John 10:11). The Word also says that He is the way, the truth, and the life. Colossians 1:16, 18 says, "For by him were all things created, that are in heaven, and that are in earth, visible and invisible, whether they be thrones, or dominions, or principalities, or powers: all things were created by him, and for him: And he is before all things, and by him all things consist of. And he is the head of the body, the church: who is the beginning, the firstborn from the dead; that in all things he might have the preeminence."

The Persistence of the Word

We usually separate our daily responsibilities and activities and our relationship with God from each other. However, we should invite God in everything that we do. Our blessings and rewards come from Him, not men. This means that we should live a life to please God. Here is how the Amplified Bible describes Colossians 3:23–24: "Whatever may be your task, work at it heartily (from the soul), as [something done] for the Lord and not for men, Knowing [with all certainty] that it is from the Lord [and not from men] that you will receive the inheritance which is your [real] reward. [The One Whom] you are serving [is] the Lord Christ (the Messiah)."

What Is This Word Saying to You?

6

WORD SEEDS THAT FIGHT SPIRITUAL BATTLES

WHETHER ONE LIKES IT OR NOT, THERE IS A SPIRITUAL BATTLE that's taking place in heaven and on earth. The fight is between good and evil, God and Satan. All of mankind is affected by that war. The foremost enemy of God is Satan. He is also the enemy of mankind and is doing everything that he can to prevent men, and women from being saved and living the abundant life that is realized in salvation. The Bible says that Satan accuses man before the Lord day and night (Revelation 12:10). First Peter 5:8 reminds us that he is as a roaring lion who seeks to destroy and devour anything that he can. All lies are a direct result of his leading. He is called the father of lies in John 8:44.

Satan is aware that all men are instinctively moved by their emotions. Consequently, he uses the tactic of fear in order to undermine and threaten man's faith in God. His first known temptation occurred in the Garden of Eden. His strategy was to play on the emotions and reasoning of Eve. The account of this temptation is recorded in the third chapter of Genesis, where he used fruit to appeal to her sense of beauty and her desire to become wise. She seemed to be inquisitive about the wisdom that she believed she would receive after eating the fruit. Therefore, she ate the fruit and invited Adam to eat as well, and he did. Both were able to see that they were naked immediately after eating the fruit. They hid from God when He came into the garden (Genesis 3:1–7).

Another of Satan's tactics is to try to get man to succumb to reasoning instead of faith. Faith is closely related to the emotions because it comes from hearing the Word of God, making it a function of the soul. However, faith responds to the revealed knowledge of God's Word and triumphs over reasoning. Reasons require looking at situations from a logical perspective, regardless of what God's Word says. The battle is real for those who put their faith in God. However, Jesus has given every Christian the authority to pray in His name. He has also sent the Holy Spirit to lead and guide into all truths. Reasoning cannot overcome the Word of God.

Doubt is another tool Satan uses to undermine confidence in God's Word. He is aware that man is mainly governed and controlled by emotions, urges, wants, and instincts. His strategy is to influence those areas because he is aware that they are controlled by fear. He tries to use doubt to confuse those who lack confidence in God's Word, knowing that confusion can lead to apprehension and distrust. Doubt can be alleviated by prayer and meditation in the Word of God.

Fear, Doubt, Reasoning, and Unbelief

The enemy's strategy is to pull people into fear, doubt, reasoning, and unbelief. Fear usually results in worry, anxiety, apprehension, and unease. Those are factors that cause depression (Proverbs 12:25). Worry, anxiety, apprehension, and unease working alongside doubt and unbelief can lead to sin. Fear also results in immobilization of both natural and spiritual life. Fear can also be a snare (Proverbs 29:25). A snare is a trap or a noose that will choke confidence and hinder faith. When fear, doubt, and unbelief try to ensnare, the action to take is to remember that God is with us and fighting on our behalf.

Some forms of fear, doubt, and unbelief may be rooted in how we perceive and react to outside influences. These influences may include family, friends, society, or simply the need to flow with the crowd. The voice in each of the categories may be loud, controlling, and very influential. A lack of confidence may cause one to compromise his own set of beliefs and personal desires in order to become part of the status quo. That is when prayer and the Word are needed for intervention.

Fearing the unknown is another mitigating factor that heightens doubt and unbelief. Our lives are beset by trouble, heartache, calamity, disease, death, and other catastrophic circumstances. Don't allow your five senses to control your thinking. Seek God's Word when you are overcome by fear and doubt. You will soon come to a point where His Word has overcome and become more real than what you can see, taste, hear, smell, experience, or feel.

Removing Fear, Doubt, Reasoning, and Unbelief

We have been discussing through this book that God's Word goes through a process called seedtime and harvest. The seed of faith must be planted in the heart so that it can be cultivated until the harvest comes, because faith comes by hearing the Word of God. This means we cannot have faith if we do not receive the Word of God. The Father knows all of our needs, and He says He will supply them (Philippians 4:19). It is our responsibility to exercise our faith in His Word.

No one is invulnerable to fear, doubt, and unbelief. Those emotions happen to us all. The important thing is to learn how to counter them. We can do this by making the Word of God the central focus of our existence. Meditating on and studying Bible scriptures cause passages in the Word to come alive in the heart. Word Seeds become part of the inner soul and spirit, causing conduct and actions to come into alignment with God's will. The important thing to remember is that the Word of God prevails over every circumstance.

The Lord told Joshua that he would prosper and succeed in life if he studied the scriptures and obeyed them. He commanded him to speak the Word, meditate on it continually, and be obedient to what it said (Joshua 1:8). This is His will for all of our lives. He wants His Word to be in our mouths, in the mouths of our children, in the mouths of their children, and for generations to come until His return. His Words are not empty; they are life and prosperity to the soul.

Living by faith doesn't mean that we ignore what's happening in our lives. It means we choose to let the Word of God become our primary focus, knowing that the Lord is greater than anything we are going through (see Ephesians 3:20). It also gives confidence that God is good and wants only what is best for our lives. It also implants a level of trust in the heart that will provide peace in times of suffering and hardship.

The Word declares that Jesus is the manifold wisdom of God. Everything that God wants us to know concerning Himself, including His will, acts, ways, promises, and plan of salvation, were manifested in Christ Jesus. He is the personal Word of God. The

Word represents His character. It is piercing, active, and discerning. It also brings life and healing to all who yield to it in faith.

Word Seeds have answers to any situation that may arise in the life of the believer. As discussed in the introduction, the answer is immediate in some situations. However, some seeds may need time to grow. This requires faith. Storing the Word Seeds establishes deep faith. Acting on faith produces positive outcomes. This is confirmed in the principle of seedtime and harvest.

Because the Word of God is seed, it is always looking for a place to be planted. Planting comes through knowledge. Knowledge of who God is provides revelation of His Word. That revelation releases supernatural energy and provides power to rise above challenges that are faced in life. Pleasing God provides blessings and assures that one lives an abundant life.

Hebrews 11:6 tells us that we cannot please God if we do not have faith. The Word Seeds in this book provide some practical ways to move toward a stronger faith in the promises of God. Increase your faith by reading, meditating on, and praying the Word Seeds. Many of the promise are for specific purposes. Search for Word Seeds that you can pray over any situation. Your faith will grow with each answer to prayer. Memorizing key scriptures in the "Word Seeds" will help you face situations with trust and peace. It will also increase your faith.

THE POWER OF SPEAKING FAITH-FILLED WORDS

Word Seed: "Death and life are in the power of the tongue" (Proverbs 18:21a).

The Seed of the Word

The words you speak have the ability to give life to a person or a situation. This was established when God spoke this world into existence by the power of His words (Genesis 1:1–3; Hebrews 11:3). Words can kill or destroy a person or a situation. That is because words are more than just sounds coming from our mouths; they have real power to build up or tear down, to motivate or discourage, to lift people up or to drag them down. The most negative or harmful words are usually spoken when an individual feels angry or unjustly treated. The important thing to remember is that we are going to have to give an account of what we say when we stand before the Lord, so we must learn to tame our tongues (Matthew 12:34–37).

The Action of the Word

There is supernatural power and life in God's Word, the Bible. First John 5:14–15 reads, "This is the confidence we have in approaching God: that if we ask anything according to his will, he hears us. And if we know that he hears us—whatever we ask—we know that we have what we asked of him." The first thing God wants us to do when facing any unmanageable situation is to begin to speak His Word over it! Ephesians 6:17 tells us to "take up the sword of the Spirit, which is the Word of God!" The Lord has given us His words to speak during various situations. Trust that it will work on your behalf by finding the promise of God in the Bible concerning whatever you need and speaking it out with faith and authority, knowing that it will not return void or empty but shall accomplish God's Will (Isaiah 55:11).

The Persistence of the Word

God's Word is His revealed truth. "For the word of God is living and powerful, and sharper than any two-edged sword, piercing even to the division of soul and spirit, and of joints and marrow, and is a discerner of the thoughts and intents of the heart" (Hebrews 4:12). The Word can pierce deep into our souls and bring conviction of our need to trust Christ. It is impossible for doctors and surgeons to operate on the mind or will of man. Those are spiritual problems and must be taken care of by spiritual means in order to change the heart of man. However, God's Word speaks to the deepest needs and cleanses the most corrupt heart as He drives conviction into our hearts and souls. "Nothing in all creation is hidden from God's sight" (Hebrews 4:13a).

What Is This Word Saying to You?

WE CAN LIVE IN PEACE IN THE MIDST OF STORMS

Word Seed: Jesus says, "Peace I leave with you; my peace I give you. I do not give to you as the world gives. Do not let your hearts be troubled and do not be afraid" (John 14:27).

The Seed of the Word

Choosing to receive peace requires trusting the Lord and giving Him both our hearts and the emotions that try to overwhelm us. When we give Him our hearts, He saves us from anything that we face by lifting the darkness around us, bringing us into the light of His glory, and allowing His peace to overrule the anxiety and frustrations that try to overwhelm us. We are justified with God through the death of Jesus. Being in right standing with Him brings us peace, grace, joy, and love. We no longer must fear the wrath of God against sin, because they have been forgiven in Jesus Christ our Lord.

The Action of the Word of God

"Thou will keep in perfect peace those whose minds are steadfast because they trust in you" (Isaiah 26:3). Sometimes the ground we stand on begins to crumble and shake, causing us to begin to worry and fret. These are the times when we must remember who God is and all the things that he has done for us. This includes the storms He has saved us from and the storms that He has pulled us through. Trusting in the Lord is believing in Him and His Word, realizing that He is all-knowing, all-powerful, and present everywhere. He is also our unchangeable, eternal rock and strength. We find peace when we trust and rely on Him.

The Persistence of the Word of God

What we think about God will determine what we do with our problems. King David wrote the following: "The LORD is my light and my salvation; whom shall I fear? The LORD is the strength of my life; of whom shall I be afraid" (Psalm 27:1). He did not focus on problems when he was surrounded by them. Instead, he focused on God. Significantly, he focused on the adequacy of God to help him deal with his problems. He did not cry out, "What am I going to do?" Instead, he cried out, "What is God able to do?" His faith in God came through a life of living in the furnace of difficult experiences. He learned through those experiences that God was bigger than his problems. He also understood that when God was with him, his adversaries and enemies were not able to prevail against him.

What Is This Word Saying to You?

THOU PREPAREST A TABLE BEFORE ME IN THE PRESENCE OF MY ENEMIES

Word Seed: "Thou prepare a table before me in the presence of my enemies" (Psalm 23:5).

The Seed of the Word

This scripture is reviewed from David's experience as a shepherd. The shepherd prepares the meadow or grazing land for the sheep. In doing so, he finds a pasture that is appropriate for the sheep to eat, relax, and browse. Just as he watches over and cares for the sheep, the Lord arranges for the life and circumstances of the believer to be peaceful and fulfilling. Psalm 37:23 (NLT) informs us that the Lord will direct the steps of His people. He delights in every detail of their lives. There is no other god like Him; nor can there be one like Him. All power and authority are His. He alone gets involved for the good of the believer, in all circumstances and in every way.

The Action of the Word

As a shepherd, David understood that when sheep grazed, they would be bothered by gnats and flies buzzing over their heads. The purpose was to try to lay eggs in the tissue of the sheep's eyes and nasal passages. The eggs could inflame the mucous membrane and cause harm to the sheep. Shepherds were trained to pour oil over the sheep's head to prevent this from happening. That is the meaning of the head being anointed with oil. The Lord anoints believers with His Holy Spirit (1 John 2:20). The anointing of God's Spirit in the life of the believer is there to console and to remove fear, doubt, and unbelief. The resulting feelings would be peace and joy (Isaiah 61:3). Knowing the Lord as our refuge prevents doubt and unbelief.

The Sufficiency of the Word

Christians can feel overflowing joy, love, and peace in the Lord. That is why Apostle Paul advises us to be filled with the Spirit (Ephesians 5:18b). We cannot be filled with the Spirit when we are already filled with sin, arrogance, or willfulness. The Christian must be willing to empty himself of those characteristics and anything else that would hinder the Spirit operating in his life. The corresponding blessing would be the Holy Spirit's freedom to accomplish His will, causing an overflow of blessings. God's grace knows no limits and is sufficient to meet all our needs (2 Corinthians 12:9).

What Is This Word Saying to You?

THE LORD IS ALWAYS WITH US!

Word Seed: "Though the fig tree may not blossom, Nor fruit be on the vines; Though the labor of the olive may fail, And the fields yield no food; Though the flock may be cut off from the fold, And there be no herd in the stalls—Yet I will rejoice in the Lord, I will joy in the God of my salvation. The Lord God is my strength; He will make my feet like deer's feet, And He will make me walk on my high hills" (Habakkuk 3:17–19).

The Seed of the Word

No matter what season we experience in life, the Lord is always with us, seeing and taking interest in every situation. And just as He knows us and everything about our lives and circumstances, the Lord wants us to get to know Him better so that we can lean on His strength and ability as we go through life. When Jesus left to go back to the Father, He left word that He was and always would be with His people (Matthew 28:20). To assure this promise, He sent the Holy Spirit to teach, bring truth, nurture, strengthen, lead, guide, reassure, and empower each believer for godly living. And no matter what the conditions and outcomes in life, His grace is sufficient to meet all needs and take care of every circumstance, resulting in peace and prosperity (Romans 8:28).

The Action of the Word

Prophet Habakkuk (Habakkuk 3:17–19) went from complaining to confessing joy during a season of his life where he experienced fear, doubt, and unbelief. He had learned to listen to and wait on the Lord as he prayed for revival in the land and to restore the salvation of the people (read the entire book of Habakkuk). Waiting on the Lord is not always easy. It can be a time of testing and loneliness. However, Habakkuk was willing to persevere in faith until the Lord came to fulfill His promise. The fulfillment of a promise may not always come in our lifetime, or it may come in a different manner than expected. However, trusting the Lord will bring peace and gladness of heart, for the joy of the Lord in our strength (Nehemiah 8:10).

The Persistence of the Word

No matter what devastations dominate our lives, Jesus can bind up the brokenhearted and transform fear, doubt, and unbelief to praise. He is always with us, waiting to comfort and bring joy and contentment to our lives and circumstances. Importantly, He restores peace and calm to the fearful and brokenhearted, and He rejoices over His own with love.

What Is the Word Saying to You?

JESUS DEFEATED THE POWERS OF SIN AND DEATH ON THE CROSS TO GIVE US PEACE

Word Seed: "Do not be surprised at the painful trial you are suffering, as though something strange were happening to you, but rejoice that you participate in the sufferings of Christ" (1 Peter 4:12–13a).

The Seed of the Word

Apostle Peter helps us to understand that some suffering is designed to refine and help us mature in the Christian faith, not to harm or weaken us. In summation, he was saying fierce trials will come; don't let them surprise you. Jesus didn't return to heaven and leave the believer without support on earth. His assurance, spoken before He ascended to heaven, was that He would be with each believer forever (Matthew 28:20). This assurance should comfort those in fear, doubt, and unbelief concerning the Lord's care for His own. He will never leave or forsake those who follow His Word. Most important, the believer can expect that the spirit of glory and of God (1 Peter 4:14) will rest upon and strengthen during times of hardship and trials.

The Action of the Word

Jesus defeated the power of sin and death on the cross. In Him is the fullness of life and peace. Therefore, when we are in the middle of sorrows, trials, and sufferings, we can take heart and have peace in Him. He didn't tell us that we would experience a life of peace, calm, and freedom from trial. In fact, He made us aware that our lives would be filled with trouble. But His ending Word was that every test and trial would be overcome (John 16:33). This should bring comfort and joy to all. It should also help many to understand that the challenges of life do not have a scheduled agenda; neither does the Lord send a memo to inform when they will happen. They just occur unpredictably and without warning. In some instances, the outcome may be devastating. The purpose of trials and tribulations is to test the faith of the believer. It is certain that they leave worries and sorrows in the heart. However, no human being on earth can escape hard times or tribulations; they are part of life and are there for a divine purpose ... to test the faith of the believer (James 1:2–4, 12).

The Persistence of the Word

Striving to become like Christ is not an easy task; neither does following Him assures one of a life of ease. Jesus reminds us in John 16:2 that following Him might even lead to cruelty and injury; some may even be martyred. But thanks be to God that every trial brings victory through Christ Jesus. That is why it is essential to always have the Word of God to guide, the Holy Spirit to enable, and the presence of the Lord to come to in prayer and for fellowship.

What Is This Word Saying to You?

VENGEANCE BELONGS TO GOD

Word Seed: "Beloved, never avenge yourselves, but leave it to the wrath of God, for it is written, 'Vengeance is mine, I will repay, says the Lord'" (Romans 12:19 ESV).

The Seed of the Word

Our key scripture informs us that we are not to avenge ourselves when people actively work evil against us, but we are to leave the matter to God. God sees all and knows everything. One day there will be a judgment, and everything will be brought to light and exposed (Revelation 20:12). No work will be overlooked (Romans 2:6). We may ask, "But what about now? I need some intervention right now." Believers cannot become vengeful people but are to be loving and forgiving (Ephesians 4:32). Importantly, they must remember that all justice is in the hands of God (Romans 12:19). There is no need take revenge because the Lord will. The directive is to live a just life, love to bless others and have mercy on them, and to fellowship with the Lord (Micah 6:8).

The Action of the Word

Almighty God will right all wrongs committeed against His people. Apostle Paul underestood this when he wrote to the Thessalonians ((2 Thess. 1:6-10) and told them that God was just. He also informed them that the Lord would recompense those who caused the trouble. In order to fully understand this statement, we will need to understand the relationship between justice and righteouness. Justice is making things right that are unfair in society; righteousness is doing right by people. Justice flows from God's heart and character. Rigteous is who He is. Our responsbility is to forgive those who have wronged us and leave justice to God. We must also repent and make relationships right where we have been at fault.

The Persistence of the Word

God gives three requirements for those who choose to seek, serve, and worship him: to act with justice, love mercy, and walk in a fearful and revential manner with Him (Micah 6:8). How does one act justly? By behaving with an upright moral character and seeing others from the perspective of God's Word. Walking humbly means to go about life doing right because the Word of God says so, knowing that the reward of righteous living results in blessings and honor. Walking humbly with the Lord means walking in a way that honors His authority and sovereignty.

What Is This Word Saying to You?

THE POWERS OF THE WRITTEN AND SPOKEN WORDS

Word Seed: "All Scripture is God-breathed and is useful for teaching, rebuking, correcting and training in righteousness, so that the servant of God may be thoroughly equipped for every good work" (2 Timothy 3:16–17).

The Seed of the Word

The Word of God is an eternal and enduring seed that is intended to be sown into the heart of man. In Matthew 13:1–23, Jesus compares the Word to seed. He describes the soil that receives the seed as the heart of man. The Word will take root in our hearts when we read and meditate on it, listen to good teaching, pray, and allow the Holy Spirit to lead and guide us. When we allow the Word of God to be sown in our hearts, everything that the Lord has spoken in scripture will achieve the purpose God ordained it to accomplish.

The Action of the Word

Proverbs 18:21 informs that death and life are products of the tongue. It would be wise to time the tongue at all times. If it is not checked, it will produce death and toxic outcomes. The tongue is small, but it is immensely powerful. When the Holy Spirit is allowed to control the tongue, it brings blessings and gives life. Controlled by the Holy Spirit, it blesses, refreshes, and gives life. Many of us have spoken words in our lives that we wish we could take back. A lot of the unwise words and comments have brought death, destruction, and ruin. That's probably why the Bible says so much about the tongue. Importantly, words reveal who controls our heart. Ephesians 5:17–20 commands us to be continually filled with the Holy Spirit. A life filled with the Holy Spirit pours out blessing and praises to God. Endeavor to let the Holy Spirit take control of what you say.

The Persistence of the Word

God is the living God, and His Word cannot be separated from Him. Therefore, the Word that we read in the scriptures is "living Word." The Holy Spirit is the doorkeeper of God's Word, and God watches over His work to perform it. That means He guards and keeps watch over the scriptures. To man, the soul and spirit seem to be the same. But the Word of God can discern between these two. Therefore, the Word has the power of God to separate every thought into good and evil. Importantly, it provides everything we need to know the difference between righteous acts and deeds and unrighteous acts and deeds.

What Is This Word Saying to You?

CHRIST RESTORES: HE MAKES CROOKED PLACES STRAIGHT

Word Seed: "I will go before thee, and make the crooked places straight: I will break in pieces the gates of brass, and cut in sunder the bars of iron: And I will give thee the treasures of darkness, and hidden riches of secret places, that thou mayest know that I, the Lord, which call thee by thy name, am the God of Israel" (Isaiah 45:2–3).

The Seed of the Word

The crooked place can be a place of deceit, stubbornness, pain, ignorance, or distress. It can also be a place where one has been struggling in a certain area of life for some time. When crooked places are made straight, obstacles are removed, mountains (such as disease, divorce, loss, financial difficulties, heartaches, addictions, and other conditions of life) are removed, sins are forgiven, lives are redeemed, and we receive grace to go on. The Lord may remove the mountain altogether. If you are at a point where fear, doubt, and unbelief are trying to burden you down, just remember that the Lord can lead you to a high mountain, where you can receive His glory. Jesus took Peter, James, and John up to a secret place for his Transfiguration. They saw His glory as a bright light; it came from within. They also heard the voice of God calling Jesus His Son (Matthew 17:5).

The Action of the Word

John the Baptist was the voice in the wilderness, urging the people to repent of their sins to look for the coming of the Lord. Isaiah (40:3–5) prophesied that valleys would be exalted, mountains and hills would become leveled, the uneven would become straight, jagged places would become smooth, and the glory of the Lord would be revealed when the Lord came. The glory of the Lord was revealed at Christ's birth. His death and resurrection redeemed men from the clutches of sin and spiritual death. Just as He sent John the Baptist to proclaim salvation to the people, the Lord goes ahead of us in every plan and journey in our lives. This includes the difficulties and obstacles along the way. When He is allowed to lead and guide, impossibilities become possible. Most important, He will make the warped and twisted paths straight. The uneven places will become smooth, he will level every mountain and valley in our lives, and He will fill us with His glory. He will cause those who have what you need to release it to you.

The Sufficiency of the Word

Today's key word encourages us not to be afraid in whatever situations we find ourselves. It also reassures us that if we trust in the Lord, He will see us through. The important thing to remember is that every challenge has an expiration date. God is faithful, and He is our ever-present help in times of need. He has given us His Word, so as not to be fearful, because He is always with us. We can rest in this promise. Another reassuring promise found in 1 Corinthians 15:33 says that no temptation can overtake our blessings. Trust God and let His Word remove that fear, doubt, and unbelief in your life, that you may be able to bear it.

What Is This Word Saying to You?

OUR SUFFICIENCY IS IN THE LORD

Word Seed: "I can do all things through Christ who strengthens me" (Philippians 4:13).

The Seed of the Word

The key scripture is not a promise that believers will have superpowers or that they will be immune to the challenges in life. The focus is that God has the ability to meet our needs, that He can help us during times of plenty as well as when we have great needs. That is why Paul was able to say that the Lord will supply all of the needs of His own, according to the blessings that come because of Christ Jesus (Philippians 4:19–20).

The Action of the Word

Each believer's needs and desires are completely satisfied in the person of Jesus Christ. He has sufficiently saved us, He has blessed us with all spiritual blessings, and He has sufficiently empowered us to live a victorious life. When a person receives Jesus Christ as Lord and Savior, he enters into an all-sufficient relationship with Him, because He is an all-sufficient God. Importantly, God's grace is able to make all grace present to abundantly bless him (2 Corinthians 9:8).

The Sufficiency of the Word

Just before Jesus ascended to heaven, He told His disciples that He would send a Helper, the Holy Spirit, who would live in, teach, and guide all those who believe in Him (Acts 1:5; John 14:26, 16:7). Spiritual discernment is the ability to tell the difference between truth and untruth, and it comes from being sensitive to the promptings of the Holy Spirit. Our minds become renewed to spiritual things when we study and meditate on the Word of God (Romans 12:2). The written Word of God can give you general direction. However, for specific discernment, you must be able to recognize the voice of the Holy Spirit and be sensitive to His promptings. You can be certain that the Spirit will never lead you into doing something that is opposite of God's written Word, because the Holy Spirit and the Word always agree. Romans 8:14–15 tells us that those who are led by the Spirit of God are sons of God. To be led by the Spirit is to obediently follow His leading as our sovereign, divine guide. We do not have to pray to be led by the Spirit. However, we need to follow His voice willingly and obediently.

What Is This Word Saying to You?

PUT GOD FIRST

Word Seed: "But seek first the kingdom of God and his righteousness, and all these things will be added to you" (Matthew 6:33).

The Seed of the Word

Fear, doubt, and unbelief bring unnecessary baggage and work. Every day, we are faced with choices and opportunities to put our time and energy into things that are temporary and have no lasting spiritual value. If we are not careful, fear, doubt, and unbelief can take up much-needed space in our hearts and minds. If not regulated, they entrench themselves into the soul and cause depression and anxiety. The top priority of any believer should be a relationship with God. Believers should fight against anxiety by focusing on the Word of God and fellowshipping with Him in prayer and praise. Pursuing His kingdom must be the main priority. He will take care of the other needs in our lives.

The Action of the Word

Trusting God to direct our path with all our heart is being able and willing to go wherever God take us. That is because we cannot see what is ahead or down the road, but God can. He knows us better than we know ourselves. Significantly, God knows what we stand in need of, and He alone can supply all our needs, according to His riches in glory in Christ Jesus. The most important thing to realize is that the Lord is our strength and shield. His strength is unending, and His shield cannot be penetrated. He is with us, for us, and all around us. He builds us up in the inner man and protects us from external harm and danger.

The Sufficiency of the Word

It should be all of our goals to have a deep, intimate relationship with God. That means that we must invite Him into every area of our lives. Serving God with our whole heart and making Him first in our lives will cause us to prosper and be at peace with ourselves as well as with others. Not putting God first in our lives is like finding a priceless jewel, and instead of wearing it or selling it to make a profit, we place it in the back of the dresser drawer and never think about it again. The key is to lean on the Lord every day, more than anything else. When we do that, we make Him our rock, our fortress, our Savior, and our deliverer. He becomes the place of protection for us. Most important, the Lord will give us grace to do what is needed in our lives.

What Is This Word Saying to You?

CHRIST WILL FINISH HIS WORK IN YOU

Word Seed: "I am sure of this, that he who began a good work in you will bring it to completion at the day of Jesus Christ" (Philippians 1:6).

The Seed of the Word

God is busy working in the Spirit to complete His plan for His people, even when they are not aware that it is happening. Paul is saying that that the Lord will finish the work that He started in the life of the believer on the day of salvation. He not only has the will to be with the redeemed, but He desires to fellowship with them. That knowledge should leave one with faith, confidence, and hope, because when the Lord starts a work, He completes it. He had a plan for each of us before we were born. He also wants the believer to know that He will work all things according to His will and their good (Romans 8:28).

The Action of the Word

Believers are saved from the darkness of the past and forgiven of past sins. God planned for, initiated, and provided salvation through the death of His Son, Jesus Christ, on the cross. The root meaning of the word *sanctify* means to set apart. The Lord God sanctifies and sets us apart through the operation of the Holy Spirit as He leads and guides into the truth of God's will and Word. Importantly, the Holy Spirit works to bring one into spiritual maturity and growth. The responsibility of the believer is to rest in His love and yield (live in obedience) to His work in the inner man. Because that is the point where spiritual maturity starts to happen.

The Persistence of the Word

Resting in the finished works of Jesus happens when an individual stops laboring in his own works and comes to the realization that he needs God to work for him. Christ died on the cross in our place and for our sins. His love and grace make it possible to enter into a real and personal relationship with Him. There is nothing more that can be added to make anyone more worthy to receive His promises and blessings. His sacrifice and love were enough. Your faith afforded you the privilege of His grace. If you do not believe that you are blessed with every spiritual blessing in Christ Jesus, then you will work and never rest. In fact, you will become exhausted and frustrated, tying to live the Christian life. You must have confidence in God's Word and His will to bless you and give you an abundant life. Christ offers us inner rest. And He will be our righteousness, identity, security, and priority. We must have faith to believe that.

What Is the Word Saying to You?

SALVATION AND THE NEWNESS OF LIFE

Word Seed: "The thief comes only to steal and kill and destroy. I came that they may have life and have it abundantly" (John 10:10).

The Seed of the Word

Christ was not merely speaking of the natural or material things of life when He spoke the words in the key scripture. He was speaking of the abundant life that is offered to mankind as a result of His death on the cross. Living an abundant life will be accomplished under any circumstance, whether one is rich, poor, or middle class. To live the abundant life is to have a supernatural relationship with God through Jesus Christ. It is a life that is empowered by His Holy Spirit. It is a life that will not be stolen by fear and worry but is centered on the blessings of God. The Lord designed that type of lifestyle to overcomes turmoil, troubles, and distractions. As Paul stated in 1 Corinthians 2:9, we will never be able to comprehend what He has prepared for us.

The Action of the Word

In a world that is filled with so much misery, depression, unhappiness, confusion, frustration, unfulfilled dreams, abandoned dreams, and futile efforts, believers in Christ must have firm beliefs that they can live lives of peace, joy, love, and fulfillment. That is because the presence of God's Holy Spirit is within the heart of the Christian. The presence of the Holy Spirit helps to defeat enemies, conquer fears, and drive anger, bitterness, and anxiety away. Prominently, the Lord is able to provide blessings beyond our comprehension (Ephesians 3:20).

The Persistence of the Word

Once you have accepted the gift of salvation, you are a new creation in Christ. Being a new creation means desiring a relationship with God rather than gratifying selfish desires (Ephesians 4:22–24). After coming to Christ, an individual undergoes a sanctification process. Sanctification is allowing the old, sinful nature to die. A new godly nature takes its place (Colossians 3:9–10). This life process begins and ends in faith. You will experience God's work in your life, and He will enable you to receive the abundant life that He promised you (John 10:10). Galatians 2:20 explains this in more detail by helping us to understand that salvation changes one into a believer who has received all of the benefits of salvation that Christ derived when He sacrificed His life on the cross.

What Is This Word Saying to You?

YOU MAY NOT BE HAPPY ALL THE TIME, BUT YOU CAN ALWAYS HAVE JOY

Key scripture: "My brethren, count it all joy when you fall into various trials, knowing that the testing of your faith produces patience. But let patience have its perfect work, that you may be perfect and complete, lacking nothing" (James 1:2–4).

The Seed of the Word

The joy of the Lord is as a well of water that has a bottomless supply of anointing and joyfulness. Isaiah 12:3 helps us to understand that being joyful in the Lord ushers one into His presence. When this happens, one experiences joy, peace, and blessings, even in the midst trials and persecution. The Lord will test the faith of the believer. The test will offer the opportunity to gain spiritual perseverance. Perseverance will cause one to have the stamina and peace to endure the situation with confidence and security. Importantly, the presence of the Lord will be experienced throughout the time of adversity. The experience is related to building physical muscles. The weightier the experience, the larger the muscle becomes. Spiritually, the greater the trial, the greater the joy. That's because trials always have a timeline. The endpoint always brings victory. Faith, coupled with the wisdom experienced by going through the trial, teaches one how to lean on and depend on God. The reward is always greater than the experience. Most important, the joy of the Lord provided the strength to go through. So the next time you experience hardship or undergo a trial, draw some joy from the Lord by praising Him and receiving His goodness and mercy.

The Action of the Word

We are on a journey of faith, and each of us must run our assigned race. There are many circumstances in the Christian life that can impede our progress. Instead of looking at those circumstances, we should keep our focus on Jesus. When we keep our focus on Jesus, we will not grow weary and lose heart. Remember, the Lord is a rock and fortress. He will bring deliverance into every situation. He is also a high tower and looks out for our good (Psalm 18:2).

The Persistence of the Word

Happiness is a good and positive emotion that brings satisfaction, contentment, and fulfillment into our lives. However, happiness is dependent on external sources. It is usually temporary and ends when an event passes. Joy is a spiritual connection with God that is internal. It is a fruit of the Spirit and is manifested by peace, accompanied by hope, and based upon trust in God. Let's always pray to the God of hope to fill us with His joy and peace to overflow (Romans 15:13).

What Is This Word Saying to You?

YOU HAVE REACHED YOUR TURNING POINT: IT IS TIME FOR A DECISION

Key scripture: "This is what the LORD says: 'Stand at the crossroads and look; ask for the ancient paths, ask where the good way is, and walk in it, and you will find rest for your souls.' But you said, 'We will not walk in it'" (Jeremiah 6:16).

The Seed of the Word

We all come to crossroads in our lives where we have to make decisions. Most decisions are diluted with fear of the unknown. This causes worry and doubt. Worry and doubt only lead to wasted time and lack of peace. The time spent worrying could be replaced with prayer and reading the Word of God, because that is where we will meet Jesus at the crosswalk of decision-making. Our scripture for today points to three things we need to do during this time: 1) Stand and look back at where we have come from, reflecting on how God brought us out. 2) Ask and walk. Pray to God. He will show you the best way. 3) Rest or refuse. It takes more than reading or hearing the Word of God. You have to actually be obedient to what God tells you and walk therein. This may cost initial sacrifices and lifestyle changes, but the end is life and peace (Psalm 37:7; Ecclesiastes 7:8; Romans 8:6).

The Action of the Word

Just because a certain path or course of action seems right, that is no guarantee that it is right. And just because another path may not seem to be the one to take does not mean that it wrong. The Bible warns us that the way of man ends in death (Proverbs 14:12). That is why one must trust in the Lord and not lean to his own understanding or insight. God knows the end from the beginning, and He will lead us in the way that is best.

The Persistence of the Word

One of the most important decisions that we can make is to not let worry and anxiety control our lives. This may seem difficult because life constantly surrounds us with conditions that can cause us to be fearful and overanxious. But God wants so much more for us than to walk through life full of fear, worry, and anxiety. He did not promise us that He would do every single thing that we request. But He does promise to give us peace that will rise above and go beyond our problems.

What Is This Word Saying to You?

7

CULTIVATING PEACE

We LIVE IN A STRESS-FILLED WORLD WHERE EVERYONE experiences turbulence from time to time. Thankfully, one of God's promises is that He will provide us with His peace in the midst of trouble. Jesus promised that He would leave us His peace (John 14:27). We read in Philippians 4:7 that the peace of God guards the heart during trouble and spiritual warfare. He is an ever- present deliverer who will always help us to experience victory when we trust in Him and walk in His peace.

Conflict is not new. It has been a part of man's world since the Fall of man in the Garden of Eden. The Fall caused sin to come into the world, corrupting the natural world and everything that is a part of it. Sin is behind every spiritual battle. The spiritual battle is between good and evil. It is an unseen war between God and Satan. It is also a battle to destroy the soul of man.

Spiritual battles are fought in the spiritual realm, the natural realm, and in the hearts and souls of men. That includes the spirit of man, body of man, and the soul of man. God's Word is used as a sword by the Holy Spirit to transform situations that war against the spirit, body, and soul of man. Jesus is the Word. He sent His Word as seed to save and set free from the grips of sin. And only one spoken Word is needed to destroy the enemy. This implies that every time a Word Seed is spoken, mountains become plains, battles are won, storms calm and dissipate, the captives are removed from imprisonment, and angels hear and respond to God's commands (Psalms 103:20).

Peace guards hearts and minds during adverse situations (Philippians 4:7). This peace is desired by all, because spiritual battles usually begin in the mind. God's peace protects man from the onslaught of the battle. He wants man to live free from worry, anxiety, and fear, to live in peace. His peace (the peace of God) provides security from catastrophic events, rage, spiritual warfare, and natural warfare. *Strong's Greek Lexicon*[20] uses the word *eirēnē* to describe this peace.

Peace is a powerful weapon. It is part of the armor that is used to wage spiritual battles and referred to as the Gospel of peace in Ephesians 6:15: It is also a fruit of the Holy Spirit (Galatians 5:22–23) and an attribute of God that enables the Christian to live in harmony with the Word of God. In other words, it is an attribute that the Holy Spirit will produce in us. The kind of peace is not an external peace, nor does it depend on circumstances. It came only live in the heart of man.

Peace is always available when the presence of God is near. This is confirmed in Philippians 4:13, where Paul conveys to the body of Christ that all things can be done through Christ when one is obedient to His Word. Honoring the Word of God through obedience results in peace and confidence. They are products of God's blessing (Psalm 25:10).

Almost of apostle Paul's epistles began with a greeting that included the words *grace* and *peace from God*. Along with being a fruit of the Holy Spirit and a spiritual weapon, peace is also a gift from God. It provides quiet and tranquility of mind, and that goes beyond human understanding (Philippians 4:7). James says that drawing close to be brings Him near to us (James 4:8). The closeness comes from a life that trusts in God. Psalm 91 blesses us by proclaiming that dwelling or living in the presence of God equates to being in a secret place that is surrounded and protected by God's goodness. It is a meeting place. It is also a place where one can hide from worries and adversities and live in peace.

Being at peace does not mean that one will not be surrounded by hardship. It means we will not experience the outcome of the hardship. It means walking with God in the midst of the storm. It means experiencing His quietness throughout the storm. It means that we are eliminating the lies of the enemy. It means that the Lord is crushing Satan (Romans 16:20).

Walking in peace and being victorious in life comes from relying on Jesus Christ. He was victorious over death, sin, and the devil. The Lord is the God of Peace (Romans 16:20; Hebrews 13:20). And He invites us to come to Him for rest (Matthew 11:28–30). Meaningfully, man is to look to Him when challenges arise. He promises to keep those who trust in and lean on Him in perfect peace (Isaiah 26:3). That means He offers a continual state of inner calmness when we trust in Him to see us through our storms.

Jesus invites us to draw close to Him. He promised that He would draw close to us as well. He is a refuge during times of trouble (Psalm 46:1). It is our prayer that you experience that peace and presence of the Lord Christ as you allow the Word Seeds to usher you into His presence. Listen to His voice as He speaks to you through His Word. The Word will still storms and quiet troubles.

The Word Seeds also offer fellowship and companionship when you simply want to converse with the Father and Son through the Holy Spirit. The table of the Lord is spread for you to feast in His presence.

CONTENTMENT

Key scripture: "For I have learned to be content whatever the circumstances" (Philippians 4:11b NIV).

The Seed of the Word

Discontentment can produce an emptiness in one's life that cannot be satisfied. That is because contentment is not something that we find in things, people, or circumstances. Contentment is related to faith and has to be learned or experienced through testing. James 1:3–5 helps to explain how faith is tested. Significantly, he assures that the fruit of patience always replaces the spirit of fear. The Lord knows and is well able to meet all of our needs. Don't allow fear to have dominion in your life. God's perfect love never fails when you rest in His truth. It important to fix your eyes on Jesus and trust His Word in every situation.

The Action of the Word

First Timothy 6:6 explains that living according to God's will is a critical factor that is needed for contentment. This is a God-centered life. A life that is God centered is filled with gratitude. Living in gratitude for what the Lord has done leads to godliness. Gratitude and contentment go hand in hand. Gratitude is being thankful for what you have. Contentment is being satisfied with what you have. Contentment is a source of inner peace. Philippians 4:6–7 describes how being thankful and grateful lead to the reduction of fear and anxiety in every circumstance in life. This does not always lead to worry-free lives. It means that prayer and thanksgiving are the keys to peace.

The Persistence of the Word

Apostle Paul found the secret to the Christian life through going through trials. He revealed in Philippians 4:11-13 that his past experiences taught him that God's peace was always present in the lives of believers. And no matter how hard the situation or circumstance, the Spirit of peace will always surround believers. Paul also realized that he had to die to himself in order to live for God. This knowledge helped him understand that the Lord has a specific calling and purpose for the life of each believer. This type of calling dictates suffering and adverse experiences. The Lord guarantees peace and contentment to anyone who makes the decision to trust and follow Him.

What Is This Word Saying to You?

HOPE

Word Seed: "May the God of hope fill you with all joy and peace as you trust in him, so that you may overflow with hope by the power of the Holy Spirit" (Romans 15:13).

The Seed of the Word

We can understand from the key scripture that God is called the God of hope. He is the source of all hope, joy, and peace. The three characteristics originate from and are found in the power of the Holy Spirit. Faith is important in all of this. Faith comes from the Word of God. The love of God and the Word of God are needed for hope. We are connected with God by the love that was revealed through the gift of Christ to us. The love of God motivates us to have hope (1 Corinthians 5:14–15). Love also provides a confidence hope of eternal salvation. Meaningful knowledge of God's love makes one certain of the fulfillment of His promises. We can rejoice in that knowledge.

The Action of the Word

Hope is not wishful thinking. It's confident, expectant, and joyful knowledge that God is with us, and we will one day see Him face-to-face. Just as an anchor stops a ship from drifting with the winds and currents of the ocean, hope keeps our eyes fixed on the throne of God. Believers have a living hope in the Word of God. His Word is faithful. His promises are true. They can always be trusted to come to pass. God is faithful and true in everything that He says and does (2 Peter 1:4). Having this hope anchors the soul. Outstandingly, trusting in Christ equips one to live a full life of joy and peace.

The Persistence of the Word

It is easy to get discouraged when going through trials and sufferings. But no matter how difficult the pain and distress, no matter how bitter the situation may become, no matter how pressing the problems bearing upon us, we can only find peace and rest in God. Psalm 62:5–7 helps us to understand that one can always have hope and security in the Lord. Christ is our rock and salvation. Abiding in Him will always still the storms of life. He is the eternal security that provides a fortress of hope, protection, and love to the suffering by calming fears and stilling worried thoughts. The fortress of His love would be our eternal protection.

What Is This Word Saying to You?

TAKE AND POSSESS WHAT IS YOURS

Key scripture: "I am giving all of it to you! Go in and possess it, for it is the land the Lord promised to your ancestors Abraham, Isaac, and Jacob, and all of their descendants" (Deuteronomy 1:8 NLT).

The Seed of the Word

Before Israel took possession of the Promised Land, God told them it was available to them. He gave them a description of what it looked like and gave it to them as a gift. The children of Israel did not actually possess the Promised Land until they went in by faith and possessed it. This is true in all situations. God's will for the believer is health, prosperity, and peace. The enemy is determined to hinder God's will by trying to produce sickness, anxiety, poverty, and fear in the lives of believers. It is essential that believers have a knowledge and understanding of their inheritances (promises) and how to possess them. God's promises do not automatically operate in the life of a believer. One must have knowledge and an understanding of those promises and then claim them by faith. Reading and trusting God's Word and asking Him for knowledge and understanding are requirements for claiming His promises (James 1:5–6). He knows what each person has need of and when to fulfill His promises. He will always provide the best for each of us.

The Action of the Word

God's promises do not always automatically operate in our lives. Before Israel took ownership of the Promised Land, they had to possess it and make it their own. They had left the wilderness and entered the borders of Canaan. But they had to actually across the boundaries into Canaan before possessing it. If we want what God has for us, we have to go possess what He says is ours. We do this by having a knowledge of His Word through reading, prayer, and meditation. Believers must also have faith and belief in the power of the Word to execute what it says it will perform. Faith and belief have the same root meaning, which is to take God at His Word and to trust and believe that what His Word says is true. The third ingredient for possessing the promises of God is to act on the Word. If our beliefs do not line up with God's Word, then we will have to change them, for God's Word is truth. He will do what His Word says (Jeremiah 1:12). Then we must obey His commands.

The Persistence of the Word

God's promises are real and are found throughout the Bible. They are not only promises but statements of what is already ours (1 Peter 1:3). Psalm 119:165 teaches that peace and safety are found in the Word of God. Peace comes from loving God and obeying His Word. Safety is provided when one is not offended. *Easton's Bible Dictionary*[21] defines an offense as an injury, or a stumbling block, or temptation. The blessings of the Lord will always prevail the work of the enemy. No offense or stumbling block can keep one from being blessed by God. Nor can the offense cause one to stop serving God.

What Is This Word Saying to You?

LIVING A LIFE OF PEACE, OBEDIENCE, AND ABUNDANCE

Key scripture: "If we ask anything according to His will, He hears us. And if we know that he hear us, whatsoever we ask, we know that we have the petitions that we desired of him" (1 John 5:14–15).

The Seed of the Word

Jesus taught His disciples to pray for God's will to be done the same on earth as it is in heaven in Matthew 6:10: God's will is His Word. His Word contains His promises of living an abundant life. God cannot lie; His promises stand firm (Titus 1:2; Isaiah 41:10). However, many of His promises come with conditions. The key scripture is one of them. Let us review a similar scripture, John 15:7: This scripture helps us to understand that the power of the Word of God is the source of His will. It also instructs that believers are to make the Word a living source of their thoughts, actions, and spoken words. Importantly, remaining and abiding in God's Word glorifies Him. In summary, abiding in God's Word means to live in Him, get to know Him, depend on Him, be obedient to His Word, and allow His Word to transform the life. When those happen, faith to receive His promises is acted upon and achieved.

The Action of the Word

Psalm 119:2–3 helps us to understand that God will not allow anyone to compromise His Word. He does not want anyone to knowingly express anything that does not align with what is written in the Bible. Nor does He want His people to deviate from what His Word says. These areas of compromise are sinful. They cause maliciousness and confusion. The way to peace is found when Jesus is made the way, truth, and life of one's life. Believers must take time to search the scriptures until the Holy Spirit guides them into the truth of God's Word.

The Persistence of the Word

The abundant life began at salvation. It is more than wealth, prosperity, and riches. It is an overall blessed life that is empowered the by Holy Spirit and provides exceedingly abundant blessing far better than we could ever imagine (Ephesians 3:20). The thief is the destroyer in our lives who comes to steal our joy and peace by trying to prevent us from receiving the full blessings of salvation. Jesus Christ came to free us from the bondages of sin and to provide us with a life of peace, joy, fulfillment, and abundance here on earth.

What Is This Word Saying to You?

RESTING AND PROSPERING IN THE LORD

Key scripture: "Beloved, I wish above all things that thou mayest prosper and be in health, even as thy soul prospereth" (3 John 2).

The Seed of the Word

Strong's Greek Lexicon [22] describes the Greek word for prosper (euodoō) to mean to succeed; or to help on the road, to succeed in reaching, to succeed in business affairs, to have a successful journey, or to lead by a direct and easy way. It can be concluded that prospering every area of life includes being successful and well in the spirit, soul, and body. This is God's will for man. The premises is that prosperity means more than money and the accumulation of wealth; it also means an ongoing state of success that touches every area of man's life. Christ died so that we may be saved from sin and delivered from oppression and suppression. He also died so that His people are preserved in health until His return. This is the abundant life that He spoke of in John 10:10.

The Action of the Word

Isaiah 40:31 promises that those who wait or rest in the Lord shall find strength to overcome. King David was an overcomer. However, he had to wait approximately fifteen years from the time Samuel first anointed him to become king over Judah until he actually overcame the battle for kingship and reigned as king of Israel. If the entire book of Psalms is searched, one would find many instances where David waited on the Lord. He summed up his waiting during those times in Psalm 62:5. It was there that he explained that waiting on the Lord was a time when he would quiet his soul. He expressed that his expectation was to always hear from Him. That is the Lord's will for all, to wait in quietness and seek to hear His voice (Psalm 37:7). His answer will always be on time (Isaiah 55:11).

The Persistence of the Word

Jesus invites all who are struggling with burdens and cares of this world to come to Him for peace and rest. He is speaking of rest for the soul (Matthew 11:28–29). Rest for the soul is more than rest from physical tiredness. This rest is focused on the cares and burdens of this world. Those are what weigh on the heart of man. Jesus's offer was to ease soul burdens and replace them with His rest. We spend too much time meditating on problems—rolling them over and over in our minds, worrying, trying to figure out how things should work out. We need to realize that worrying is useless! It is said that worrying is like sitting in a rocking chair. One rocks all day. At the end of the day, there is no movement from the starting position. We must come to Christ and find peace and rest in Him.

What Is This Word Saying to You?

THE CONQUERING POWER OF GOD'S GRACE AND PEACE

Word Seed: "Grace and peace be multiplied unto you through the knowledge of God, and of Jesus our Lord" (2 Peter 1:2).

The Seed of the Word

The Lord places an extremely high value on the believer's ability to pursue and receive spiritual knowledge (see 2 Peter 1:3). Proverbs 8:13–14 explains that gaining knowledge is greater than obtaining all the silver, gold, and material things of this world. Importantly, having a sure knowledge of the Word of God is the only sure way to gain personal peace. This truth is confirmed in Romans 5:1–2. Paul explains in those scriptures that accepting Jesus Christ as Savior justifies a Christian. The result of justification is having peace with God. This makes one a son of God and a joint heir with Jesus Christ (Romans 8:17). The result is that the Christian is at peace with God.

The Action of the Word

Grace and faith work together. Grace is God's undeserved favor bestowed on those He has called to salvation (Ephesians 2:4–10). Grace is available to every believer. Growing in grace is accessed by faith. Faith is acting on the Word of God because you believe it is true. Christians who operate in the faith of God are not looking at what they see but are looking at what God's Word says about the matter. Christians believe that Jesus is the Son of God. They believe that they are heirs of God's kingdom. And they believe that through the power of the Holy Spirit, they have power to conquer sin and evil (1 John 5:4–5). These are the unmerited blessings given to all believers because of their saving relationship with the Father and Son.

The Persistence of the Word

Strong's Greek Lexicon [23] describes grace by the Greek word *Charis*. Charis means favor or blessings. The blessing of the Lord makes one to be in a position to lack no good thing from Him. Grace is God's favor toward mankind. That means that the believer is saved by God's favor. To be saved means to be delivered, protected, preserved, healed, and made whole. Favor guarantees God's presence and provisions in the lives of His people. He not only blesses His own, but He also shines His light and forms a protective presence over them (Psalm 5:12). This brings peace that cannot be comprehended with the human mind.

What Is This Word Saying to You?

GROWING IN FAITH AND PLEASING GOD

Word Seed: "But without faith it is impossible to please Him, for he who comes to God must believe that He is, and that He is a rewarder of those who diligently seek Him" (Hebrews 11:6).

The Seed of the Word

Christians please God and are justified by faith in Christ as the Savior who died for their sins (initial salvation). But once saved, Christians are to please Him by being diligent and by living by faith. *Strong's Greek Lexion* [24] uses the Greek term *ekzēteō* to describe the meaning of diligently seek. It means to seek out or to be persistent in learning and obeying God's will in all areas of life. Jesus challenges Christians to be diligent and to obey Him. He calls for the total commitment of His followers in Matthew 16:24–25. He asserts in this scripture that it is impossible to love and obey Him and to desire the things of the world at the same time. Obeying God brings blessing now and in the eternal. Loving the world and the dictates of the worldly culture is temporary. The outcomes is soul damnation.

The Action of the Word

Believers are saved and justified by their faith in the atoning death of Jesus Christ. This makes them at peace with God (Romans 5:1). Being at peace with God means we can be in a personal relationship with Him. This is an eternal peace. In addition to receiving peace with God, Christians gain access to His grace. Jesus removed all the barriers between God and His people when He died on the cross. This gives Christians free access into God's presence for eternity.

The Persistence of the Word

Ecclesiastes 12:13 informs us that the greatest purpose in life is to fear God and to be obedient to His Word. All of God's will for mankind is found in His commandments. The commandments in God's Word guide the Christian. They show them how to make a God-centered lifestyle their choice and to inform them of God's will for every area of their lives. God's Word explains the benefits of obeying the dictates in the Bible and discusses reprimands and retributions that come with being disobedient to its laws and dictates. The Bible was written by man, but it was inspired by the Holy Spirit (2 Timothy 3:16). Christians are reminded in Philippians 2:12–13 to be constant and committed to the practice of obeying God's will. They are also reminded to be faithful to His calling. Actions of obedience and conformity to His Word are rewarded by God (Hebrews 11:6).

What Is This Word Saying to You?

CULTIVATING THE FRUIT OF PEACE

Key scripture: "Finally, brethren, whatsoever things are true, whatsoever things are honest, whatsoever things are just, whatsoever things are pure, whatsoever things are lovely, whatsoever things are of a good report; if there be any virtue, and if there be any praise, think on these things" (Philippians 4:8).

The Seed of the Word

Peace begins from within and affects everything that surrounds you. That is because what we spend our time on shapes us and those around us. When we fix our eyes on God, He strengthens us and gives us His peace. Being at peace does not mean you have a perfect life. Instead, it is an emotion that comes from how you deal with everything around. Peace is a constant when you learn how to control fears, release resentment and complaints, remove negative thoughts and worries from your mind, and let go of things that you cannot control. Focusing on the Word of God is focusing on the goodness of God. He is the one who will bring peace to the soul.

The Action of the Word

Peace is prevalent when the heart and the mind are focused on the truth of God's Word. Peace will cast off the cares of the world while it stands guard at the door of the hearts and the mind. The Lord gives the power and supplies the strength to go through any ordeal in life. His peace will bring calmness and rest to the soul. Feeding on the Word of God and the blessings of His goodness, rather than the circumstance of life, will help one stay focused on God's love. In other words, saying no to evil and negative thoughts will cause the truth of God's Word to give strength and rest.

The Persistence of the Word

Prayer brings one into God's presence. Being in the presence of God brings peace. Peace is not always the absence of problems. It is the joy and calmness experienced by being in the presence of God. There are two types of peace: peace with God and the peace of God. Peace with God means that our sin debt has been paid and God sees us as righteous. The peace of God comes when we move away from the world and toward God, knowing that He will always hear and answer prayers of faith (Mark 11:24; 1 John 5:14). Learn to experience God's peace.

What Is This Word Saying to You?

INDEX

ENDNOTES

Chapter 1

1. "Logos," *Merriam-Webster.com Dictionary, Merriam-Webster,* https://www.merriam-webster.com/dictionary/Logos, accessed November 30, 2022.
2. John Heslop-Harrison, "germination," *Encyclopedia Britannica,* August 29, 2022, https://www.britannica.com/science/germination, accessed September 17, 2022.
3. Hans Lambers, "seed," *Encyclopedia Britannica,* September 22, 2021, https://www.britannica.com/science/seed-plant-reproductive-part, accessed November 30, 2022.
4. "H3372 - yārē' - St*rong's Hebrew Lexicon (kjv)."* Blue Letter Bible. Accessed 11 Apr, 2023. https://www.blueletterbible.org/lexicon/h3372/kjv/wlc/0-1/, accessed December 3, 2022.
5. Mason, Keith, ed. *King James Online Bible Dictionary.* N.p. https://av1611.com/kjbp/kjv-dictionary/doubt.html.

Chapter 2

6. Vine, W. "Meditate - Vine's Expository Dictionary of New Testament Words." Blue Letter Bible. Last Modified 24 Jun, 1996. https://www.blueletterbible.org/search/Dictionary/viewTopic.cfm.

Chapter 3

7. Vine, W. "Wisdom - Vine's Expository Dictionary of New Testament Words." Blue Letter Bible. Last Modified 24 Jun, 1996. https://www.blueletterbible.org/search/dictionary/viewtopic.cfm.

Chapter Four

8. Vines Expository Dictionary - Salvation." Blue Letter Bible. Web. 7 Oct, 2022. <https://www.blueletterbible.org/search/Dictionary/viewTopic.cfm>.

9. Pink, Arthur. A Four - fold Salvation: *Resurrection from the Penalty, Pleasure, Power, and Presence of Sin* (California: Create Space Independent Publishing Platform), August 26, 4014, 14 pages.

10. Ibid.

11. Ibid.

12. Vine, W. "Sin (Noun and Verb) - *Vine's Expository Dictionary of New Testament Words.* Blue Letter Bible." Last Modified 24 Jun, 1996. https://www.blueletterbible.org/search/Dictionary/viewTopic.cfm.

13. *"G1656 - eleos - Strong's Greek Lexicon (kjv)."* Blue Letter Bible. Accessed 11 Apr, 2023. https://www.blueletterbible.org/lexicon/g1656/kjv/tr/0-1/.

14. *"G5485 - charis - Strong's Greek Lexicon (kjv)."* Blue Letter Bible. Accessed 11 Apr, 2023. https://www.blueletterbible.org/lexicon/g5485/kjv/tr/0-1/.

15. *"G4991 - sōtēria - Strong's Greek Lexicon (kjv)."* Blue Letter Bible. Accessed 11 Apr, 2023. https://www.blueletterbible.org/lexicon/g4991/kjv/tr/0-1/.

Chapter 5

16. "G38 - hagiasmos - Strong's Greek Lexicon (kjv)." Blue Letter Bible. Accessed 11 Apr, 2023. https://www.blueletterbible.org/lexicon/g38/kjv/tr/0-1/.

17. "G601 - apokalyptō - *Strong's Greek Lexicon (esv)."* Blue Letter Bible. Accessed 11 Apr, 2023. https://www.blueletterbible.org/lexicon/g601/esv/tr/0-1/.

18. "Dictionaries - Wait." *Blue Letter Bible.* Accessed 11 Apr, 2023. https://www.blueletterbible.org/search/Dictionary/viewTopic.cfm.

19. "G26 - agapē - *Strong's Greek Lexicon (kjv)."* Blue Letter Bible. Accessed 11 Apr, 2023. https://www.blueletterbible.org/lexicon/g26/kjv/tr/0-1/.

Chapter 7

20. "G1515 - eirene - Strong's Greek Lexicon (kjv)." Blue Letter Bible. Accessed 11 Apr, 2023. https://www.blueletterbible.org/lexicon/g1515/kjv/tr/0-1/.

21. *"Dictionaries - Offence." Blue Letter Bible. Accessed 11 Apr, 2023. https://www.blueletterbible.org/search/Dictionary/viewTopic.cfm.*

22. *"G2137 - euodoō - Strong's Greek Lexicon (kjv)."* Blue Letter Bible. Accessed 11 Apr, 2023. https://www.blueletterbible.org/lexicon/g2137/kjv/tr/0-1/.

23. *"G5485 - charis - Strong's Greek Lexicon (kjv)."* Blue Letter Bible. Accessed 11 Apr, 2023. https://www.blueletterbible.org/lexicon/g5485/kjv/tr/0-1/.

24. *"G1567 - ekzēteō - Strong's Greek Lexicon (kjv)."* Blue Letter Bible. Accessed 11 Apr, 2023. https://www.blueletterbible.org/lexicon/g1567/kjv/tr/0.

WORKS CITED

List of Recommended Reading

Barron, Robert. *Seeds of the Word: Finding God in the Culture*. Des Plaines, IL: Word on Fire Publisher, 2016.

Burke, Dennis. *How to Meditate God's Word*. Tulsa, OK: Harrison House Publisher, 1982.

Evans, Tony. *Praying through the Names of God*. Eugene, Oregon: Harvest House Publisher, 2014. https://www.harvesthousepublishers.com/data/files/excerpts/9780736960519_exc.pdf.

Hickey, Marilyn. *The Names of God*. New Kensington, PA: Whitaker House Publishing, 2009.

Krow, Don. *How To Meditate on God's Word*. Rogers, AR: Don Krow Ministries, 2004. https://delessons.org/tools/de_program_condensed/Level_2/02_How_to_Meditate_on_God's_Word_condensed_version.pdf

Hemphill, Ken. *The Names of God*. Nashville: Broadman & Holman, 2001.

Martin, Catherine. *Trusting in the Names of God: Drawing Strength from Knowing Who He Is*. Eugene, Oregon: Harvest House Publishers, 2008.

Packard, J.I. *Knowing God*. Downers Grove, Il: InterVarsity Publishers, 1973.

Stone, Nathan. *Names of God*. Chicago, IL: Moody Press, 1994.

Spangler, Ann. *Praying the Names of God: A Daily Guide*. Grand Rapids, Michigan: Zondervan, 2004.

Spangler, Ann. & Tverberg, Lois. *Sitting at the feet of Rabbi Jesus; How the Jewishness of Jesus Can Transform Your Faith*. Grand Rapids, MI: Zondervan, 2009.

Sumrall, Lester. *Faith Can Change your World*. Whitaker Distribution: Virginia Beach, VA: Whitaker Distribution, 1984.

Wommack, Andrew. *God's Word – the Seed of His Blessing*. Colorado Springs. CO: Andrew Wommack Ministries, 2023. https://www.awmi.net/reading/teaching-articles/gods_word/.

Printed in the United States
by Baker & Taylor Publisher Services